The Coffee Chased Us Up

ELOF NORMAN

The Coffee Chased Us Up

MONTE CRISTO MEMORIES

THE MOUNTAINEERS

Copyright© 1977 by The Mountaineers,
719 Pike Street, Seattle, Washington 98101

First printing, March 1977

Manufactured in the United States of America

Published simultaneously in Canada by Mountain Craft
P.O. Box 5232, Vancouver, B.C. V6B 4B3

Library of Congress Catalog Card No. 77-722-54

ISBN 0-916890-48-1

Cover/title art by B.J. Packard

To Isabella

Foreword

The importance of a ghost town lies not so much in what it is today as in the way it stirs the intelligent, inquisitive visitor to try to imagine what the town was like in the period of its greatest activity. And yet it is not easy to visualize fully and accurately the life and bustle and spirit of its boom days. For example, how can one, viewing a skeleton, picture the body that once encased it; how can one know the character and personality — the love and laughter of the individual it represents?

To Elof Norman, the few ramshackle buildings of today's Monte Cristo are not merely the remnants of a ghost town. Rather, they are keen reminders of the community he knew so well in the days of his youth: a town he loved, a town with warm and human relationships, with days of rumor and excitement interspersed with days of disappointment and hard existence.

Elof Norman recognized that he was among the very last survivors of those who could remember Monte Cristo at its best. What's more, he realized that here was a story that should be recorded — and recorded well. To the credit of this quiet, modest man it is worth noting that at the age of 75, Norman, a retired tavern owner, enrolled in a private creative writing class conducted by Zola Ross. He did this so that he could learn the writing skills that would enable him to present his story factually and graphically and as good reading.

In telling of his boyhood in Monte Cristo, Elof Norman has — in truth — told the story of scores of boys and their families who lived in scores of western mining towns in boom times. For that we can be grateful to him. The indebtedness of readers in future years will even exceed ours, as the fairly recent past of our time becomes the distant past of theirs. For here is a notable contribution to Americana.

Robert Hitchman
President, Washington
State Historical Society

Contents

Monte Cristo

An epitaph to a memory

I look upon this place today
and wonder what I'm going to say.
The time has gone, the years have passed,
but memories linger to the last.
The miners' hopes were on the gold they sought
while braving the hazards they all fought.
They now have left, their houses stayed,
so lonely — where once we played.
Those homes have vanished, crushed by snows,
the tired victims of Nature's blows.
The peaks still stand, so rugged and steep,
hiding the gold they seek to keep.
Now tourists come to gaze in awe,
and ponder at what the miners saw!

  Elof Norman

1

"Swede Foreigner, Swede Foreigner!"

It was the 24th of June, 1902. We were on a rickety train crossing the Cascade Mountains in the state of Washington. It had been a tedious and uncomfortable journey for my mother, Petra, my sister Ely, age five, and myself, age eight. Twelve days on the steamship Oscar II, cooped up in the steerage compartment, sleeping in wooden bunks three tiers high, crowding in line to get a dish of ill-prepared food. Those fortunate enough to have lower bunks could sit down to eat, but with no chairs or tables, others ate where they could. Our one small bunk was the highest, where all three of us slept.

Then Ellis Island, to be pushed and shoved to different places, and questioned. Tags were pinned to our clothing with instructions for where we were to go. Waiting and sleeping on benches in depots was the usual thing. Food was a problem, too, although our mother had some black coarse rye bread in a bundle she carried. We ate some food at counters in depots, although trading four krone for one dollar was expensive.

All that was in the past. This was to be the last day of traveling. We had arrived in Hartford, Washington, the night before. We stayed with a Scandinavian speaking family that night. That was the first time we had had a chance to take a bath, change clothes, and sleep in a bed for nineteen days. We were lucky our two trunks had come too.

We were now on the last leg of our journey. Today we were going to see our father, Otto Norman, who had come to America some two years before and had settled in the mining town of Monte Cristo. He had sent us $200.00 for our fare, which was almost gone now.

"Are we really going to see our father today?" Ely asked.

"Yes, Ely," our mother said. "Your father will be there to meet us. Remember, in the last letter he wrote, he had a house all our own. It will be wonderful to have a home all to ourselves here in America."

"Mama, may I have a piece of bread?" asked Ely. "I'm hungry."

"Oh, you're always eating," I said teasingly. "You'll get fat and no beau will look at you."

"Never mind, Elof, she has lots of time," Mama said, and reached into the bag for some dark bread.

Over the bridges and through the tunnels, the train continued on its way, sometimes going very slowly around the sharp curves, with the wheels squealing shrilly on the sharpest ones.

Other passengers, some dressed very well, showed signs of recognizing places as we got closer to the destination. Feeling jovial, a few tried to speak to us. The language was strange to my mother and Ely, but I had had some instruction in English in school in Denmark. I had a little understanding of words, but did not always use the right ones or pronounce them correctly. The other passengers talked to me only to hear me reply, then to chuckle or smile a little at my obvious mistakes. I realized it was just in fun, so I didn't mind.

The train soon came into the mountains. It followed the rushing river on one side and the towering peaks on the other. Beyond the water were other peaks. It was soon clear that we were going through a valley between mountains. The mountains came closer and closer and the valley became narrower until we stopped at a cabin with a sign, Barlow Pass. In a few minutes we continued on, with the mountains still closer. The grade must have been getting steeper, for the engine was puffing harder and going slower.

At one place the train stopped, and then it backed up for a distance on another track. We three wondered what it was all about. Soon the train started forward again, but on another and much higher level. So I realized we had been on a switchback to get higher up. The slope was too steep for the locomotive to pull the train. We were really in the mountains now.

About noon the train slowed down and some buildings could be seen. This must be Monte Cristo!! Ely and I rushed to the side of the train and peered out the window.

"It's Father. It's Father!" I shouted.

"Come and see, Mama!" Ely went to her and pulled her by the hand so she could get a first glimpse of Papa, while everyone smiled at the eagerness expressed in the Danish tongue. Then we were at the top of the iron steps, with the cinder bed still passing beneath our feet.

"Watch your step," said the conductor, holding us back.

The train came to a stop and we were in Papa's arms and he was lifting us high.

"My Petra, my Petra, that long journey has at last brought you to me."

He kissed us all to wipe away the sorrow of our separation. "Come and see the home I have made for all of you."

The numerous people at the station were welcoming us with handshakes and words of congratulation for our safe arrival.

We finally crossed the tracks away from these welcoming people, and went through a turntable-roundhouse (where locomotives were turned around) and on to a raised walkway for a hundred feet to our front porch. Then up twelve outside steps to the main floor, and we were home!

A table of food had been prepared by some of the neighborhood ladies, which was appreciated by us all. Ely and I were soon full and were anxious to explore our new home.

The house was on the lower steep slope of what was called Toad Mountain. It was two and a half stories high in front and one story high in back, with an attached lean-to woodshed, whose back door led to the customary backhouse.

The shingled roof was very steep so the snow could slide off in the winter when the lower windows were boarded up. The main living quarters were on the second floor and consisted of a living room, a combination kitchen-dining room, and two bedrooms. The top floor was empty. The lower floor, or basement, was for storing cordwood, to be cut up later into stove wood lengths, and for storing food supplies.

Standing at our front windows, Ely and I could see over the top of the turntable shed to the main part of the town. There were mountains all around us except for a small gap where the train came through. Everything was either up or down. No level spots anywhere except the train tracks. It was just like a deep bowl with the snow covered peaks surrounding us.

Later we were to learn the names of the different mountains. Facing our house was Addison Peak; to the right were Cadet and Wilmans Peaks and then our own Toad Mountain, so named because of an outcropping of rock which looks like a huge toad.

That first day, my sister and I were busy exploring around the house, looking longingly at the acres of huckleberries not yet ripe. Just imagine, we thought to ourselves, here we are able to pick berries for free. Wood had to be cut from the trees around us for the stoves, but that was free, too. How wonderful it was to have come to a place where so many things were free just for the taking.

We had already picked out the bedroom we were to share as long as we were small, and, tired of exploring, we were soon ready for our first meal that Mama had prepared in our new home. After supper we went to the two beds in the room we had picked out, for a well deserved rest and a resolve to do more exploring the next day.

In the morning we were awakened by Mama grinding coffee beans in the grinder on the kitchen wall. That was to be our alarm clock for all the years we were in Monte. Sometimes, if we were real sleepy, the smell of new-brewed coffee soon chased us up.

I was curious to see the whole coffee beans, which were new to me.

Papa had bought two one-pound bags. One bag was Arbuckle's brand and the other was Lion's Head. Lion's Head beans were cheaper, but the bag had some shriveled up and half green beans in it, so after that we only bought the Arbuckle brand.

Ely wanted to watch the chickens in the back yard. They were the first live ones she had ever seen and the clucking and scratching interested her. She also hoped the huckleberries had ripened.

I was more interested in the other houses on the same side of the tracks as we were. On the right of the turntable was a large, one-room house, in which were some Japanese. They smiled, waved, and bowed. They wanted me to come in but I did not go. I learned later they were the section crew that kept the ties and track in repair. Beyond their house was a larger building, where dances were held on special occasions. To the left and lower down was a big house with a sign which said Barney's Saloon. Several small huts were scattered around it.

There were three tracks: the main line went to the depot, and also split off to a side track for boxcars to be unloaded. The third track went to the water tower and the turntable.

I did not have time to look anymore, because I saw a group of boys approaching from across the tracks. I walked toward them, when suddenly they threw some rocks at me. I ran quickly back to the roundhouse. They continued to throw more rocks and yelled, "Swede foreigner, Swede foreigner!" I found some rocks and threw them back at the boys. I must have aimed pretty good, because they ran back across the tracks and uptown.

I told my father about the rock throwing when he came home. He just laughed and said, "That is just the boys' way of getting acquainted. They were testing you. When you threw rocks back at them, they knew you would stand up for yourself. They will be good friends. You'll see."

"But, Papa, what did they mean when they hollered 'Swede foreigner'?"

"Oh, that's because we are from another country. They think all Scandinavians are Swedes. Everything will be all right. There won't be any more rocks thrown."

A few days later I was again crossing the tracks to go up to the main part of town when two boys, who had been rock throwers, came toward me. As they came nearer I saw they were smiling so I knew they wanted to be friends.

We didn't understand everything we said, but that didn't make any difference. Their names were Dan and Joe Cook. Dan was nine and Joe was seven years old. They knew my name, but Dan never did say it right. He always said Alof, with a long A, but I didn't mind. I wasn't saying the English words too good either.

After a while we went to their house, which was down the tracks away from town. We had to cross the river on the railroad trestle. Looking down I could see the rushing water under it and I became dizzy. I tried not looking down and stepped between the ties, skinning my leg. Dan said, "That's not too bad. You'll learn. Just feel with your feet. See."

Their home and three other houses were on a narrow strip of land between the tracks and the river. I met a younger brother, Claud, some smaller brothers and sisters, and their mother. We had a good visit. What I liked best was when Dan said that when he was throwing rocks a few days ago he wasn't really trying to hit me, but was only throwing because the other boys were.

I invited Dan and Joe to come to our house but they had some work to do at home. That reminded me that I had promised my mother to carry up water from our downstairs pump and to fill the wood box by the kitchen stove.

2

They Are Blowing Up the Whole Town

The biggest part of the chores around the house was bringing wood inside for the winter. I had never seen or used an axe or a saw in Denmark, so those were things to learn to use without getting hurt. My father had some trees cut down near our home. I helped him cut them into cordwood lengths and dragged them into the basement, where I could cut them up for the stoves.

As most of the woods were on Toad Mountain, Dan and Joe came to cut wood there, too. Addison Peak, near their home, had been logged off by the former sawmill and was now nearly covered by blackberries, which would soon ripen. Two other boys came, too. They were Bert and Theo Cleveland. They were about the same ages as Dan and Joe Cook. Their younger sister, Gertie Cleveland, came to visit Ely. We did not cut much wood that day; we were more interested in visiting. They wondered if I was still mad about the rock throwing. Also, they looked to see if the huckleberries were ripe. We had a good time talking and some work was done. Later we went to our house and had some newly baked cookies.

Most of the talk was about the Fourth of July and they wondered if they were going to have money for firecrackers. I didn't understand very much what it was all about, but I did not want to seem dumb, so I kept quiet. I would ask my father what it was all about.

I soon found out. On the night of July third the people uptown started shooting off giant firecrackers and guns. Ely and I were scared and ran out of our bedroom crying, "Mama, Mama, come look out our window. It looks like they are blowing up the whole town."

Papa came too and said, "Don't worry, youngsters. Some of the miners are only starting the Fourth of July early."

"What is the Fourth of July?" we both asked.

"That's the day the United States got its independence, and we will celebrate like everyone else each year."

After watching for a while we fell asleep despite the noise, vowing we would go uptown the next day to see all the excitement.

The next morning we got up early. No work, so Papa was home, too —mostly, according to Mama, getting in her way while she was busy in the kitchen making goodies for everyone who might come visiting.

There was very little excitement uptown. It was too early for the late celebrators of the night before. As usual, I filled the woodbox by the stove and carried up some water from the pump downstairs. With that done, I was eager to get uptown to see any excitement that might happen.

"Mama, can I go uptown now?" I asked.

"Ask your father," she said.

My father was in the first floor room which we called the basement, where he was doing some kind of work. I wondered if he remembered that he had promised me some money for firecrackers, so I could celebrate, too.

"Papa, can I go to the store now?" I asked, hoping that would be a hint about the money.

"Sure you can. I guess it is not too early, but be careful when the miners shoot off those giant firecrackers."

I stood there, disappointed. Papa grinned at me and said, "I suppose you want some money. Here's ten cents. Don't spend it all in one place."

I thought that was funny because there was only one place I could spend it, and that was at Kyes' store.

When I got to the store, Dan was already there and, of course, Leo Kyes, his cousin, was also there.

"Hello, Alof," said Dan, saying my name wrong as usual. "Going to buy some firecrackers?"

"Oh, I bet he hasn't got any money," said Leo, strutting a little because his father owned the store.

"I have so. See. I've got ten cents. My father gave it to me for firecrackers. I'm going to buy some now."

I looked around at all the different sizes and prices, with Leo coaxing me to buy one giant cracker for ten cents.

"No, no. I want some smaller ones so they will last longer."

"Well, here's some smaller ones. They are for ladies and babies. That's your style anyway," said Leo.

I didn't want any of those. They didn't pop very loud and sometimes only fizzled. Mr. Kyes came then and I bought some larger ones. He gave me five bundles for my dime and I was happy.

Dan hadn't gotten his money yet. He was only going to get five cents because in his family there were more children and they had to be careful with the spending.

Down the street we went and I shot off some crackers and let Dan shoot some, too. He was my first and good friend.

In front of the Royal Hotel a group of miners were lighting some giant crackers from their cigars, and the crackers made real loud noises. One firecracker didn't go off. I ran out in the street, hoping to have a big one for myself. I was just about to touch it when it exploded.

Yelling and holding my hand, I ran home as fast as I could. When I came into the kitchen crying, Mama looked right away and asked what had happened. She poured some hot water into a bowl and put my hand in it. Oh, boy, that hurt twice as much and I pulled away and yelled some more.

Papa came upstairs and scolded me for being so careless. He helped Mama hold my hand in the hot water because I was trying to get away. I was hopping up and down and Mama kept saying, "Keep still, keep still. The hot water will take the hurt away."

After a while I didn't hurt so much, so I went uptown again. I had dropped my firecrackers when I hurt my hand, and I wanted them back. A miner told me one of the boys had taken care of them. I knew he meant Dan, so I went to his house, which was down the river from town. He gave me the crackers and I gave him and Joe one of the bundles of firecrackers for saving them for me.

Later that day Ely and I shot off the noise makers. Some people came to our house and had some of Mama's goodies. Papa and the men had drinks out of a bottle. I think Papa got a little tipsy because Mama laughed at some of his antics. Some of the men started a poker game just to pass the time.

Ely was looking out of the window and said, "Look, Mama, what is that man doing? Looks like he is climbing up the tree with a rope. I wonder what he is doing that for?" Papa went over to look, too, and said the man was going to hoist up some dynamite so it would make a lot of noise. We all watched. When he was all through he lit a long fuse and ran far away. When that whole box of dynamite went off the bang echoed around and around the mountains, blowing the whole top out of the tree. When it got dark that evening, someone uptown lit some Roman candles that exploded in the sky, lighting the whole valley.

Later that evening we heard music coming from a building on the same side of town where we lived. I asked Papa what it was and he said, "Oh, that is the dance pavilion. All the women and men are having a celebration dance. It is not a good idea to go over there now. Too much drinking sometimes."

I sneaked over anyway and found other kids watching from a distance. We enjoyed the music and at times pretended to dance. Altogether we had a very enjoyable Fourth of July.

★ ★ ★

The planked main street of Monte, built on a very narrow ridge about a block long, was called Dumas. This ridge separated two streams. To the north was Glacier Creek and to the south was 76 Creek. These two came together at the lower end of town, forming the Sauk River. The main railway tracks crossed the river right there and came into town. A narrow wooden bridge crossed 76 Creek from the depot to go uptown.

The planked street and all the houses were supported by timbering on the lower side. Most of the homes and business houses were on the north side. At the end of Dumas, the ridge widened out. The dirt road on the right side of the ridge led to the schoolhouse, the assay office, and some nice homes for the mine owners and foremen. The road on the left side went to the concentrator and various mines up the mountain.

Besides Mr. Kyes' mercantile store, the other large building was the Royal Hotel and restaurant owned by Mrs. Sheedy and Jakey Cohen, a small, balding, round-bellied and jolly man. The hotel's bar and gambling tables were the main attraction. Most of the single workers in town stayed there in the numerous sleeping rooms upstairs. There always seemed to be room for the miners when they came to town to spend their hard-earned money. When they went broke, they usually bummed Jakey for a bottle of whiskey and Jim Kyes for a new pair of bib overalls, and then went back to the mines for another month or two.

There were two other saloons in town: Barney's and a nameless one which had a knifing later and was closed down. All the other houses were the homes of married couples. The only other families with children were the Kimballs, with one boy named Orville, age seven, and the Hickey family, who had two girls named Alma and Leona, age eight and six.

The berries were now beginning to ripen. That made for more work for everyone. Some of us grumbled at the extra work, but we had fun, too. With a group of youngsters all the same age or almost, play became commonplace, often with a challenge to see who could fill their pail first — partly urged on by the parents.

3

It Was So Different From Denmark

As the weeks went by, I became more and more appreciative of the beauty of our little valley. We had fresh air and clean water. The evenings were especially calm and restful after a day's work. As the sun was setting, the valley would become dark while the sun shone brightly on the snowy peaks.

Later, when the moon came up it was so light you could almost read a paper. The air was so clear and the stars looked so close and large, it was easy to imagine you could reach them from atop a tall tree.

Freedom was the one thing that could be enjoyed by all, especially by the children. Free water and free wood for the labor of cutting. The land and the houses were owned by the mine owners and no one paid rent or taxes as long as they worked at the mines. We could hunt and fish any time — there were no limits and no license required. All this freedom could be had for anyone willing to work with his two hands. What more could anybody ask for? It was so different from Denmark.

The other children and I spent a lot of time climbing the mountains and looking into some of the deserted prospect diggings. Dan had shown me how to make a slingshot and we could hit almost anything we aimed at, especially the big rats at the horse barn.

But it was not all play. Wood had to be stored for the winter's fire, there was meat to be salted down in the pickling barrels, and now the picking and canning of the ripened berries. Even with all the chores it was a happy life for the children. I was glad I had come to America.

One day a group of kids were picking blackberries around a large clump of bushes when suddenly a bear appeared from the other side. We ran away fast, but the bear just grunted "whoosh" and kept on eating berries. It did not seem very much afraid. We stopped to look and then two little cubs appeared.

"I'm going to get my uncle Jim," said Dan. "He's got a rifle. He'll shoot them and we can have some fresh meat." He went away fast.

We all stayed to watch and soon Mr. Kyes came with his .35 caliber Winchester. As he went closer to get a good shot, the bear stood up and grunted "whoosh" a few more times.

When Mr. Kyes shot, the bear fell down. The kids wanted to get closer, but Kyes waved them away, saying "Never get too close to an animal that's been shot. Sometimes they play possum and will hurt you."

After a bit the bear was still, and Kyes shot the two cubs. We all ran home with whatever berries we had, to tell of the excitement. I begged Mama to let me go back to help skin the hides off, and also with the hope of getting some of the fresh meat. Mama said, "Yes," and away I went.

Dan, Joe, and Bert were already there, all trying to help, but I suppose getting in the way more than helping. Soon the hides were off and the cutting up of the meat was next. Mr. Kyes had trouble with the bones and Bert ran home to get a meat saw from his father, who had been a butcher before he became a blacksmith. Everything went better after that. Mr. Kyes was very generous, handing out the meat to those who wanted some.

Mama was happy to have the meat but did not like the wild taste, so she soaked it in a mixture of canned milk and water overnight, which made it better. It was a busy time for the mothers with the canning and all the other housework.

★ ★ ★

One constant problem was fighting fleas, lice, and bedbugs. That was one job everyone had at Monte. We mixed up kerosene, carbolic acid, and water for a remedy. All the cracks and crevices in the walls and floors were treated, and all the wooden bedsteads had to be taken apart every week and painted with the mixture. The mattresses and bedding were hung outside when possible and pounded to shake the bugs out.

Sometimes we would be rid of them for a while, then a visitor would come and the whole thing had to be done all over again. Some people we hated to see come, but in a small community like ours, no one made enemies by showing displeasure toward anyone. Each one of us had to depend on the others in time of stress or trouble.

We had two boarders now to help with expenses. Papa was determined to put a little money away for the future. They slept upstairs and kept to themselves there or in the front room, which we seldom used ourselves.

However, having boarders made more work for our mother with the extra cooking, clothes scrubbing on the board, and ironing. It was always a long, hard day for her. She was the first one up in the morning and the last one to bed at night. Seldom did she get to sit down except to mend some clothing or darn socks or sew underthings from bleached-out flour sacks.

The stamina and perseverance of these pioneer women who followed their men to faraway places has been a wonderment to me. They were the backbone of the family and civilization. Many words have been written, but not nearly enough, of their courage and determination to overcome their hardships.

Bath night was always extra work. We were lucky. We had a bathtub, while others had to use a wash tub. Our tub was an oblong wooden box, curved nicely on the inside, which was made of copper. Water had to be carried up and heated on the stove. The tub was dragged into the kitchen from the lean-to shed and filled.

Papa was first, then me, then Ely, and Mama last, all using the same water. It was a good thing we took baths often enough so the last one in could clean up, too. We kids went to bed and I suppose Papa helped Mama dip the water out of the tub and carry it outside. The boarders had to bathe at the colored man's barber shop or at the Royal Hotel. Mama said she was not going to heat water for them, too. Washing their clothes was a big enough job for the money they were paying.

4

Boys Will Be Boys

It was a bad year for Joe Cook. Through some mischance he lost an eye from a long-handled, two-tined fork his brother Claud threw at him. The infection hurt very much and he had to wear glasses after that. He played just as hard and got into just as much mischief despite the handicap. I had lost an eye in Denmark, so I knew what trouble he had.

One day a gang of boys were traveling through some brushy under-growth and the branches were whipping back in Joe's face. I became worried about his glasses and offered to take care of them. I put them in my cap for safekeeping and forgot all about them. After a while I outran the others and climbed atop a big rock, shouting, "Here I am." The glasses flew out of my cap and could not be found.

"What am I going to do?" cried Joe. "I can't see and I might get a spanking for losing my glasses."

"Gee whiz, that's not fair. If anybody should get it, it should be Alof. He lost them," said Dan.

"I was only trying to help," I protested.

I was hard put to bring up the accident at the supper table. I didn't know what would happen.

"Aren't you hungry?" Mama asked.

"Yes. I like the stew, but something happened today that makes me feel bad. I lost Joe's glasses."

So I had to tell about how it happened. Papa said, "Well, it looks like you were trying to do the right thing. I'll go right down to Mr. Cook and he can send away to Everett for some new glasses on the train tomorrow."

Joe had another accident that summer. A bunch of kids were pushing the turntable around and riding on it while it was still spinning. Joe caught his foot between the turntable and the end of the rails, and twisted his ankle and knee. If he had not had on very heavy shoes his foot would have been broken. As it was, he limped a lot for several months. He also got a scolding for being so careless!

Leo Kyes was another boy who had problems, but they were with me. Maybe I should say that I had troubles with him. He was the one who had started the rock throwing some time back and I hadn't forgotten it.

My father had given me some money to buy a lunch pail at Kyes' store. On the way to town I met a boy, my age, whom I had seen but had not met before. We stopped to talk. His name was Orville Kimball. His home was the only one on the opposite side of the street from the other houses.

He asked me where I was going and I told him I was getting a lunch pail for my father.

"I want to go along, too," he said. "Sometimes Mr. Kyes will give a piece of candy when you buy something."

"Sure, come along."

A stray dog came by and I petted it. Talking to Orville and thinking about the pail, I did not notice that the dog had followed me into the store. Leo, who still looked upon me as foreigner, and thought the dog was mine, gave it a hard kick, sending it howling down the street.

"You shouldn't have done that," I said. "It's a nice dog and wasn't doing any harm."

"Don't talk back to me. You're only a Swede foreigner but you ought to know no dogs are allowed in the store," said Leo.

That made me real mad. I swung the pail I had bought. It hit Leo right on top of his head. He fell down, crying and yelling. Mr. Kyes came running and saw Leo was not hurt badly. He said, "I saw the whole thing and I think you two boys should get a good spanking for acting like this."

I walked out of the store with the broken pail, crying because I had now spent the money for a busted one. I had to tell Papa the whole story when I got home. He said, "I'll go back with you. We'll get it straightened out."

Mr. Kyes was very nice about it, and after some talking we went home with a new lunch pail.

I got a good lecture from Papa and from what I heard later, Leo heard some words, too. Anyway, Leo and I got along much better after that. I wondered what had happened to the dog that got kicked, and I was going to ask Papa if I could have it for my own. The next time I went uptown, I found out that Orville had taken it home and had been allowed to keep it.

One thing that had bothered me was that I was not wearing the same kind of clothes as all the other boys. They wore bib overalls and jackets. I had the same clothes that I had worn in Denmark, a suit coat with long pants or knee-length pants. Papa said I would have to wear the ones I had: "We can't afford to throw away good clothes. Wear them out first."

I could have climbed through brush and over rocks and got them torn up, but I didn't dare do that. I guess I must have pestered Papa so much that it wasn't long before I got bib overalls and jacket, the same as the other boys.

Two boys whom I had seen many times, but had not spoken to, were the stationmaster's sons. Dan had told me their names were Paul and Bill Copestick, but said, "Don't bother with them. They think they are better than we are."

I wondered about that, but when I found out that Dan and Paul had had a big fight over something, I understood better. I was still determined to talk to Paul next time I had a chance. I saw him in back of the depot one day and we had a good visit. It was not Paul who was uppity, it was his father, because I heard him say one day, "Paul, don't play with those miners' kids. They're only trash."

I told Dan about what I had heard, but he must have had his feelings hurt pretty bad because he never really liked Paul or his brother.

5

Little Games

Fall was getting nearer. The maples were turning yellow and red. The canning was done and the wood piled to the ceiling in the basement. Our thoughts now were on school, soon to start. I do not remember our first teacher's name, but she was very nice. When she found out that Ely and I were from Denmark, she spent extra time teaching us how to pronounce words properly. I learned to read and pronounce a paragraph or two. Although I didn't always understand everything I read, I could learn the meaning by reading to Papa at night, because he would explain the words in Danish. The teacher wanted to speak Danish and often would keep Ely and me after school so she could learn some words. We tried to sneak out once in a while, especially after the other kids started calling us "teacher's pets."

It was a hard life for the teachers. These were their first classes, and some of the kids were having a hard time settling down after all the freedom of the summer. They were lonesome, too, being away from their families for the first time. The mothers invited them to their homes, but since the mothers were mostly busy with housework, they were not too entertaining. I had gotten a sliver in my finger one day during recess. I went in to ask the teacher to get it out, and I found her crying, with her head on the desk. I felt sorry and told Mama about it that night. After that we invited her more often, no matter how busy we were.

We were in school the day it started snowing. The teacher had a hard time getting us to pay attention to our lessons. We thought that first snow was a treat, not realizing what a problem the winter would be with a snowfall of twelve to sixteen feet during the season. When school was out we didn't go home right away. We were all too busy throwing snowballs at each other or dodging them. But we soon had our fill and went home to our after-school lunch.

The school was one large room, much larger than what was needed for the fifteen children that first year. One potbellied stove heated the room. The children nearest the stove were always warm enough, but those in back kept their coats on until it was their turn to get seats nearer the heat. The older boys kept the fire going with wood brought in from the shed next door. A pail of water with a dipper stood near the teacher's desk. We all drank with the same dipper, colds or no colds. We held up one finger for permission to get a drink and two fingers to go to the outhouse. It took a little courage to hold up two fingers with the thermometer showing temperatures below freezing.

Above all, the teacher tried to be fair, fair in attention to work, and fair in punishment which, she regretted, was necessary at times. One teacher taught all the grades, so at times she had only one pupil in a certain grade. The subjects were arithmetic, geography, grammar and spelling. At times, endless reading aloud, stumbling over words, was a monotony shared by students and teacher alike. When it became too boring, the students, especially the boys, invented little games, all variations on how to get the best of the teacher or another student. Spitballs were the commonest missiles, which usually caused several students to get a ruler applied to the palm, hard.

One day Orville Kimball (at whose house the teacher stayed) had been especially naughty, and the teacher sent him out to the woodshed to get a stick so she could paddle his bottom. He came back with a very slender sliver of wood over a foot long. All the kids giggled and the teacher sternly ordered Orville to get a larger one. He came back a little later with a larger stick. It was a four foot chunk of cordwood. The whole class roared with laughter and even the teacher had to smile. She immediately called recess to quiet the class down and possibly control herself. Orville did not get a spanking then, but got a good scolding at home later.

I do not remember the names of all the teachers we had at Monte — just the last two, when Ely and I were the only remaining students. One, however, stands out in the memory of the children of that time. He was a substitute for a younger girl who had looked the town over and refused to stay. This gentleman, and he was a gentleman, was middle-aged. His outstanding qualities were his kindness and consideration for us all. He constantly paid particular attention to those with learning problems. Despite this, *all* the children agreed that we learned more during that year when he taught than at any other time in school. He was not very healthy and sometimes would fall asleep during recess. We came in just the same, and continued our lessons until he woke up, embarrassed. But we never laughed at him. Because he was not too well, the boys came to school early to start the fire so it would be warm when he arrived. That and shoveling the snow from the steps and other things we did were well deserved by that kind gentleman. It was a sadness to see him leave when school was over, for we believed he would not be back the next year. Mr. Kay will be remembered with kindness by all who had him for a teacher.

6

It's Those D--n Kids Again

Winter brought problems to the workers and the train crews. The miners stayed at the mines, so they continued running. The concentrator workers and others had to fight the snow, which would at times pile up two feet overnight. The snow did not bother the children, because the paths would be packed down by the people going to work and by the teams hauling supplies from the depot to the tramway terminal and the mercantile store.

Dumas was the main street for sleigh riding, mostly belly-busting. Not all the kids had sleds. I didn't, but Papa made me one without metal runners. Bert noticed I was not sliding so good. He borrowed my sled one day and when I got it back it had iron runners. He said his father, the blacksmith, had fixed them.

The big fun came when Leo brought out his bobsled. The fathers and mothers came out to watch and to caution, "Don't go too fast when you come to the bridge."

That was the dangerous place. The street made a sharp left-angle turn as it crossed the 76 Creek, and it did not pay to go too fast there. Paul went too fast one day and flew over the three-foot railing.

"Look, look, Paul went into the creek," someone yelled. "Hurry. Hurry, pull him out, pull him out."

We ran through the snow. Paul was lucky. He had landed in a pool, not hurt much but wet and cold. We helped him home, laughing and giggling until we saw Mrs. Copestick. She scolded us for letting Paul go too fast. That was funny, too, for we had nothing to do with his accident.

Theo had an accident, too. He didn't go over the railing but hit one of the uprights, cutting a bloody gash in his head. Leaving his sled, he went crying up the street to home. In about half an hour he came out again with his head wrapped up like a mummy, got his sled, and went coasting as if nothing had happened.

Someone else got a bobsled which the grown folks used. The kids watched with awe how fast they went, with the expert steering around the sharp curve at the bottom of the hill. Soon there were cries of "Give us a ride. Give us a ride."

They piled some of us in between them and went faster just to show off a little. We cried, "Be careful, be careful," and tumbling off in a snowbank, we thought it was too fast.

Moonlight nights were wonderful for sledding, with happy laughter from all. It was cold, but pulling the sleds up the hill kept us warm. The kids never seemed to tire, but the workers, with twelve hours' work ahead of them, had to quit long before the children wanted to.

Several times on clear frosty nights we hauled water from the creek to pour on the street, which made it one sheet of ice. Then we really wore out shoe soles, braking to slow us down on the curves. But our ice making was not appreciated by anyone trying to walk there. New paths had to be made alongside in the deep snow.

After a snowstorm everything would be covered up, but with all the traffic up and down the snow was packed enough for the kids. Anything went, from skis to the latest coasters and homemade bobsleds. They were really something when filled with eight or ten kids and grownups.

The trains came quite regularly despite the snow. At first they came with snowplows fastened in front of the cowcatcher, then later with the rotary plow. Sometimes slides covered the tracks, and the crew had to dynamite out the big rocks and trees before they could continue. The switchback tracks had to be partly shoveled out the entire half mile so the train could back up to the higher level. So, some days the train was late, but it always came. The trains had to get through, because they had to get turned around on the turntable in order to plow their way back to Everett.

With spring in the offing, the weather was a little warmer, with rain instead of snow. Slides tumbled down the mountains, shaking the whole community. Trees and huge rocks came, too. We wondered if the blackberries would be destroyed on Addison slope where the worst slides were. Later the trilliums popped up through the patches of snow under the vine maples.

The Japanese section crew and their Irish boss were busy leveling the tracks here and there. At several places the river floods had washed away the banks near the tracks, and huge boulders were placed there for protection. This is called riprapping.

The kids began to talk of going to the mines, where I had never been. I looked forward to it. According to Dan and Joe the cooks up there would give us some good eating.

In the meantime we were much too busy bedeviling the section crew and the train men. Bert had found the tool shed open and taken some of those large explosive caps called torpedoes, with a metal strap to fasten them to the tracks. He was going to have some fun with them when they exploded.

"Elof, do you want to have some fun, too?"

"Yeah, you bet. What are you going to do?"

"See these torpedoes? We'll put them on the track way down. One is for making the train go slow, and two for stopping it. I like to see the train crew get mad when they find out there is nothing to stop for."

We got Dan and Joe and Claud to come along, too. First we made sure Paul Copestick didn't see us or he might want to know what we were going to do, and he would tell his father.

We went far past the section gang to where they couldn't see us. We placed two torpedoes together on the track and one much further along. We hid in the bushes where we would be able to see and hear the train.

We waited for the train to come, giggling at times with anticipated excitement. Soon we heard the chugging, and the train came into sight around the curve. Then the single torpedo exploded with a loud bang. Immediately the brakes squealed as the engineer slowed the train. The train crew and the passengers poked their heads out the open windows, wondering what the trouble was. We could hardly contain our excitement.

Mr. Resigue slowed the train to a crawl. Soon the two next torpedoes went bang! bang! and the train stopped. The fireman and the conductor, with several passengers, got off. They gathered together, jabbering and waving their arms. Several people went up the track looking for something that might be wrong. This was the climax of excitement and fun for us.

We heard voices shouting, "I'll bet it's those d--n kids again. Let's continue on the rest of the way, or we'll be late for dinner at the hotel."

When the train was out of sight, we sneaked through the brush toward home, with every intention of being good boys for a day or two.

Another time, Orville got some homemade soap and we smeared it on the steep switchback track to the concentrator. When the train tried to back up the ore cars, the wheels spun around and around but didn't go anywhere. It was fun to watch the train crew wiping off the track with gunny sacks and rags, and hear them cussing those so-and-so kids while they sprinkled sand on the tracks.

No one had flown kites at Monte until I made one. There was not much wind except in the gap where the tracks were. I had flown many kites in Denmark on the white sand beaches. Soon the other boys and the men, too, were trying to fly their kites higher than the others. String was the biggest problem; it was mostly small pieces tied together, which sometimes broke. Leo was lucky. He swiped string from the spindle in his father's store. If someone's kite got away there was a scramble to get some string from the other fellow. Lots of fun and arguments but no fights.

★ ★ ★

Two trains came to Monte every day except Sunday during the peak years. The passenger train came at noon with one coach, one express car, and two boxcars with supplies for the mines. The boxcars were switched to the side track, to be unloaded later and hauled up to the tramway terminal by horse and wagon. The train crew then had lunch at the Royal Hotel, and turned the engine around on the turntable for their trip back to Hartford.

The ore train came in the evening. It brought up the empty boxcars and gondolas. After switching out the loaded ore cars from the concentrator and placing the empty ones there, the crew put the engine into the roundhouse until they went back to Everett early the next morning.

During the summer, Sunday excursion trains came from Seattle and Everett. I saw some of the boys gathering shiny ore samples and crushed concentrates of ore and putting them in small bottles.

"What are you doing with that stuff?" I asked.

"The excursion train is coming on Sunday," said Dan. "We're going to sell them to the people on the train."

"Can I get some, too?"

"Sure, why not?" said Dan. "There's plenty for everybody."

"Will they really buy this stuff?" I asked. "They can pick it up just as easy as we can."

"Sure they can, but they would rather buy it if you tell them there is gold in it. Anyway they don't know where to look."

I got busy picking up ore samples too, mostly those with pyrites of iron (fool's gold) in them. It shines like crazy but is worthless. I told Mama about it and she found some small bottles for the concentrates. Ely got into the act, too, and we had high hopes.

The excursion train came and with it my first experience as a salesman. I didn't do too well at first, but listening to the other boys, I followed suit. When an excursionist asked me if there was gold in the ore, I said I didn't know too much about it but it certainly looked good, and I generally sold some.

Some visitors went to the mines and others just wanted to look into the saloons to see the gold and silver coins piled on the gambling tables. Everyone seemed to have a good time.

I went home with $2.10 and Ely had some money. I gave my money to Mama because she had been looking at Sears' catalogue for something she wanted but didn't have the money for. Now, she and my sister could send away for what they wanted.

7

A Real Good Place To Go Fishing

School was over now and the usual work and play were ahead of us again. Dan and Joe did not care much for fishing. They preferred to climb the mountains. They took some perilous trips, to places where I refused to follow them.

Bert and Theo were like me. We enjoyed catching trout and eating them, too. We couldn't get enough of the fishing and went every chance we had.

There was no fishing at Monte because of the muddy washings from the ore concentrating mill. The nearest place was at Weedin Creek, three miles down the track. It was a small stream flowing into the Sauk River. With our fishing so often, we soon had the larger trout fished out.

The nearest other stream was the Palmer Creek, a tributary of the Stillaguamish River, and in the woods five miles away. My folks would not let me go there unless some grown men were along.

"What we need," said Bert, "is some real good place to go fishing."

Leo fingered the new rod his father had given him. "Yeah," he agreed.

"We could go to Palmer Creek," said Bert.

"Ah, you know Mama won't let us go there. It's too far," said Theo.

I asked Papa if we could go to Palmer Creek sometime. He said, "Ask the section boss if we can borrow the push car. Then we can coast down to the Sunrise Trail. That will save us a good five mile walk."

I talked to the section boss that day about borrowing the push car for a trip to Palmer Creek. After I explained that my father and some miners were going along, he agreed.

"Tell your father to come to my house to get the key for the padlock when you are going to use it," he said. "And be sure to padlock it when you leave it to go fishing."

We gathered at the depot the following Sunday. It turned out to be quite a crowd. The kids were Leo, Bert, Theo, and I. The grown people were Mr. Cleveland, Ed Dahl, one of our boarders, Papa, and, surprisingly, the section boss had invited himself. It was his push car, so why not?

We coasted to Barlow Pass, at times having to brake the wheels to keep from going too fast. At Barlow, a discussion was held. Some wanted to go through the woods to Palmer Creek and fish downstream, while others wanted to coast down the Sunrise Trail and fish upstream.

Papa and the section boss took the car down to the Sunrise trail, and the rest of us went through the woods for a half mile to the beginning of Palmer Creek. After we had cut poles from willow shrubs, we baited our hooks with worms dug at the horse barn, and were soon fishing.

Fishing was good. With no limit and no season, we kept only the larger ones. Mr. Cleveland yelled, "Be careful of those potholes, I don't want to have to jump in and fish you out."

The gunny sacks that we put the trout in were filled with alder leaves and occasionally dipped in the stream, so the trout were kept cool.

Later we met Papa and we all went down to the Sunrise Trail. After each one had counted his fish (some had over a hundred), a fire was started and the fish cleaned. The frying pan and a coffee pot were brought out. The smell of frying fish and bacon made us more hungry. We all ate our fill, washed down with plenty of coffee. The men told stories of other fishing and hunting trips. It made me feel good as I looked at the people around me, glad I was here and they were my friends. It was so much better than it had been in Denmark.

As the sunset tinted the sky, we decided to start home. The kids who had tired were allowed to ride the car as the men pushed it up the grade toward Monte. We made many other trips to Palmer Creek, but that first trip was remembered best of all.

8

The Budding Businessman

During that summer there were two things I wanted. One was to go to the mines, and the other was to own an air rifle. When I asked my father for the rifle, he looked at me very calmly and said, "You are too young to have any kind of rifle."

"But Leo has one and Paul is going to get one on his birthday," I said.

"I said no," Papa said sternly. "A dollar is too much to pay for such foolishness. We can put it to better use than that."

I knew we did not have much money, so I was determined to try in some way to earn some myself, but how in the world could a nine-year-old earn any money in a town that had only one street, and that a block long?

This little town had only seven family homes, three gambling saloons, Leo's father's mercantile store, and a couple of boarding houses.

The low-paid workers at the concentrator mill did their own errands, so the opportunity to make any money by doing errands was pretty slim. On pay day, the miners from the five mines on the mountains came to town, but they were too busy to pay any attention to the kids.

One day Leo and I were supposed to be cutting wood not far from our house when I saw a glimmer of a chance to make some money. Leo had brought a wild, wild west story book. We weren't supposed to read such "trash," but we did anyway when we were by ourselves. On the back cover I saw an advertisement that sent my hopes soaring.

"Sell jewelry and win an air rifle," I read with excitement, but when I showed it to Leo, he was discouraging.

"Yeah, I saw it," he said. "I think it is a skin game. They'll get you to sell some of their stuff and won't give you anything."

I was still determined to try, so I answered the ad without telling anyone. When the parcel came I had to tell my father all about it. I opened the package and when I saw what it contained, I was disappointed, too. There were thirty-six pieces — gold-colored stickpins and rings with colored glass in them — to be sold at ten cents apiece. It looked pretty hopeless.

My father said, "You might as well try to sell what you can in town and then go up to the mine, if you can get someone to go with you. It might be a good lesson for you not to bite off any more than you can chew."

I didn't have much luck in town. With Leo tagging along and remarking, "I told you so," I felt pretty low. I approached a miner that I knew slightly and said, "This stickpin will look good in your tie."

He laughed and gave me a dime for a pin, saying, "Why not, it's only the price of a drink."

His friend, however, gave me back the ring he had been fingering and said, "No girls here to give this to, and I never wear a tie. I'd rather have the drink, anyway."

I had only sold seven pieces in town, so the next thing to do was to go to the mines. When I asked Leo and Paul if they would go up to the mines, they said yes, and we arranged to go the next day.

We were all tired from climbing that steep rocky trail to the mines, but we arrived in good time. The miners were coming out for their noon lunch. I approached the first one, but he hardly noticed me. The same thing happened with all the other men. Leo whispered, "They act as if we weren't here. What are you going to do?"

We three stood in the dining room doorway and watched the miners eat amid shouts of laughter. But they were paying no attention to us.

Suddenly a number of explosions occurred in the tunnel. I was scared and started to run, but Leo grabbed my arm and said, "They always shoot off blasts while the men are out to eat, then the air compressor blows out the fumes before the miners go back."

As if the explosions had been a signal, the miners turned to us, and with wide grins and shouts of laughter, they surrounded us and greeted us with handshakes and slaps on the back. One loud voice stood out amongst the rest.

"You like our leetle joke? No?"

"You no like play games? Yes?"

"What you got in box? Look, gold for ten cents. Everybody buy one . . . two . . . three, we buy all of them."

In a few confused moments all the pins and rings were sold. I was glad and the men seemed happy, too. They strutted around showing off the colored stones, as if they were diamonds, rubies, and emeralds.

"Look, this diamond shines bright. I won't need any candle in the tunnel," shouted one.

"I'm going to give this ring to my best girl. See, it fits my little finger," cried another.

Then a whistle blew and the fun was over as the men went back to work, leaving three confused but delighted boys. As we were about to leave, the camp cook stopped us, saying, "You boys aren't going to leave without getting something to eat, are you? Come in and eat. You must be hungry after that steep climb from town."

The fresh meat roast and fresh vegetables were a welcome change from the salt meat we got at home. We ate until we were full, so when the cook brought some dried apple pie and peach pie and apricot pie, we wished we had not stuffed ourselves.

"Go ahead, boys," said the cook. "Fill up while you are here. This doesn't happen every day."

We managed to eat some of each kind of pie. Bert Cleveland came in just then, for he had heard we were up there and hoped he could get some goodies, too.

Bert only wanted pie, and the cook gave him a whole apricot pie. When he was through, the cook asked him if he wanted more. Bert said, "Sure, I can eat several pies." When he had eaten half of the second one, he turned to the cook and said, "I don't think you made this as good as the other one."

The cook laughed and said Bert's eyes must be bigger than his stomach.

We stayed a little longer because we were so full, but left when the cook started washing dishes. We walked slowly and talked about what we had eaten and how the miners had fun with us. I was especially glad I had sold all the trinkets. Now I could send the money away and get the air rifle.

I told my mother all that had happened at the mine and what we had eaten. She laughed and asked, "Do you think the camp cook is a better cook than I am?"

"No, Mama, you're the best cook of all. Only we ate things we don't always get."

"That's good. You can go again sometime, but don't make such a pig of yourself. Now go to the store and send the money away before you lose it."

That was one thing that was not going to happen, I thought, as I hurried uptown. When I showed the postmaster the letter and told him to send the money to the address on the envelope, Mr. Kyes said, "You can't send it that way. You have to have a money order and that costs fifteen cents."

Fifteen cents, I thought, as I hurried home. Maybe Mama has it. If not, I would have to wait until Papa came home and he was not too anxious for me to have a rifle.

Worry, worry, I thought. First worry about not selling the things, and now worry about the money order, and maybe there won't be a rifle after I send the money. Worry, worry.

Luckily, Mama had the fifteen cents. She had been saving that money to send for something from Sears, but she gave me the fifteen cents, knowing she would have to wait to get what she wanted.

While Mr. Kyes was making out the money order he asked me why I hadn't bought the rifle at the store. I told him I hadn't had a dollar, and this way I was getting a gun for doing a little work. Mr. Kyes thought that was all right and hoped I would not be disappointed when the rifle came.

The next few weeks were anxious ones. When the rifle finally came I was happy, although it was not as fancy as Leo's. It was, however, something I had earned myself, and I had many good times practicing shooting with Leo and Paul.

9

Mines and Miners

There were five mines operating at Monte when we arrived there in 1902. The Pride was on Glacier Peak and was connected with the Mystery mine on Wilmans Peak by tunnels and shafts. The Golden Cord and the Justice mines worked the other veins of ore at different levels on Wilmans Peak. The Rainey mine was close to town, and was a shaft mine with tunnels extending out at different levels. The lower levels were constantly being flooded and pumps were operating all the time.

The workers at the mines on the mountains, several miles from town, stayed at the bunk houses there. The food was good, and they paid $1.00 a day out of their $4.00 a day wages for it. The men at the ore concentrating mill received $3.00 a day, and worked longer each day than the miners' eight hours.

The ores from the mines on Glacier and Wilmans Peaks came to some terminal bunkers by way of aerial tramways. From there the ore was transported by horse-drawn iron carts on narrow gauge track to the concentrator mill.

There were two types of tramway, single- and double-cabled. The heavy cables were supported by the crossarms on poles located at certain intervals. The top cable from the Pride and the Mystery mines was stationary and acted as a track on which the flanged wheels rode. These wheels supported ore buckets as large as garbage cans, which hung down below the top cable. The lower cable, a traveling cable, acted as a haul-back and brake. The brake was on a large bullwheel at the mines. The cable system worked like a chairlift for skiers — except it was not electric! All the motive power was gravity. On the traveling cable (a continuous loop) the loaded buckets going down pulled the empty ones up. Supplies to the mine could be brought up this way. The tramway from the Justice and the Golden Cord mines had only one traveling cable, on which the smaller buckets were solidly fastened.

This cable was supported on the flanged wheels located on the cross-arms of the high poles. The brakes were also on a large bullwheel at the mines.

The drillers at the mines, who were also powder men, drilled the holes at the proper places and to the right depth. When the charges were set and fuses lit, the men left the tunnel and counted the explosions. Counting was vital in order to know there were no unexploded dynamite charges left. That was one day's work for one crew. After the compressor had blown out all the dynamite fumes, the next crew went through the same procedure.

When the ore finally reached the concentrator, the ores were crushed into fine particles, deposited on revolving, shimmying rubber tables, and then washed with sprays of water. This removed the lighter particles of rock, leaving the heavier ores. These concentrates were then loaded by wheelbarrows into gondolas and boxcars, to be sent to the smelter in Everett. When in full operation, the mill could process 250 tons of ore in a twenty-four hour day or two shifts.

The majority of the miners worked a month or two, then came to town to celebrate. For some, that meant drinking. For others, it was gambling. Generally it was also a trip to the colored man's barber shop for a good scrubbing, a haircut, and a shave.

Pay days meant the biggest crowds. Sometimes a fight would start, with a group of men crowding around hurrahing one or the other of the fighters. No one really got hurt badly. Generally the two fighters were drunk and just staggered around and swung wildly at each other until they both fell down exhausted. After a while, they would get up and stumble into a saloon for another drink.

However, one time I saw two men fighting seriously. One man had the other one down and was reaching for a rock. I ran over and kicked the rock away and pushed the top man off. He made a grab for me but I got away. The other man left in a hurry. The first man hollered, "Hey, kid, come here." I was afraid and stayed away, and after a while ran home. Later that day he thanked me, saying he was glad I had stopped him, otherwise he might have hurt the other man. The fight had really started over nothing, he said.

The miners, mostly Welsh hard-rock men, were good to the children. A nickel for one of us was not unusual. There were not many opportunities for us to earn any spending money. However, Joe Cook made a little money selling an out-of-town newspaper, especially when he could sneak into one of the saloons. Sometimes a miner would toss him two bits just to get rid of him.

When the celebrators went broke, the usual procedure was to bum the saloonkeeper for a bottle of whiskey and Jim Kyes, the storekeeper, for a new pair of bib overalls and a pound jar of Copenhagen snuff.

Then up to the mines for a few more months. Most of the time they were not feeling too well on these return trips, and would coax the tram tender to let them ride up in one of the empty ore buckets. This was not allowed, but they never quit trying.

One man, nicknamed Poker Nels, a good friend of my father, tried to get a ride in one of the buckets. Papa was tram tender at the time and said, "No, Nels. I can't let you ride. I would lose my job and you're too drunk in the first place."

"Now, Otto, we are good friends. You know I'm not that drunk. I mostly play poker. Let me ride up this one time."

"No, Nels, I won't let you."

Nels then went up to the first supporting tower, climbed it, and tried to grab the next bucket as it came by. He missed but caught the traveling cable, hanging on until the next tower. There he had to let go or have his fingers cut off. He dropped about twenty feet to the rocks below, breaking his right leg and a couple of ribs. Papa stopped the tram and ran to help him. Others came to carry him to the Kimball house because Mrs. Kimball had been a nurse. Someone set the leg, but did not do a good job. Sometime later it was discovered that his foot had been set at an angle, and the foot was twisted to one side. The leg had to be rebroken and reset. Nels was laid up a long time. A sore developed on his thigh that never seemed to heal completely, and the leg was a little shorter and Nels limped a little ever after. He did, however, go back to the mines until they shut down.

10

Victuals

Sam Strom was another good friend of my father. His home was in Darrington, where he had some mining claims on Gold Hill, across the swinging bridge from town. To make a living and money for assessment work on his claims, he came to Monte to get a job, either at the mines or at the concentrating mill. He never failed to visit our home when he was in town.

As usual he carried his well-known rifle. It was a tremendous thing and he was very proud of it. It was a single shot Winchester and was chambered for .30 U.S. cartridges. The barrel was as large as the barrel of a 12 gauge shotgun. With all that iron in the barrel, it was quite a load to pack around. Only a large, broad-shouldered man like Sam would have kept a rifle that heavy. With a handful of cartridges he could shoot it almost as fast as a repeater. It has been reported that he could hit a large spike at fifty feet. He loved to show off his marksmanship and speed if someone would furnish the shells.

On one visit to our house he had another rifle with him. It was a .22 Stevens Favorite. I looked at it with envy. He watched me as I was shooting with my air rifle and said, "Say, youngster, you shoot pretty good with that. How well do you think you can do with this .22? Put a can on the stump over there and take a shot at it."

I found an old milk can and put it on a stump about a hundred feet away. It looked too far, but when I shot, I hit it right in the middle. I guess it was a lucky shot but I felt proud anyway.

"My, that was pretty good. You'll make a marksman yet if you keep that up," said Sam. "Let's go down the track a ways. Maybe we can spot a grouse. I want to see if you are careful enough to have a rifle of your own."

We did not see any grouse and when we got home Papa was there. "I've been teaching your boy how to handle a .22," Sam said. "I think he is old enough to have a real rifle. I want to give it to him."

I looked at Papa. He grinned and winked at Sam. "I guess it's all right, Sam, if you think he will handle it safely."

Sam handed me the gun and said, "Here, take it. I'm giving it to you for being such a good shot. Take good care of it."

I was glad to have it. In thinking about it afterward, I guess from the way they acted that Papa and Sam had the whole thing fixed up beforehand. I guess Papa bought it for a present for some reason. Many shells were shot out of that rifle before it wore out. Papa often said I almost kept him broke buying shells for it, even though they only cost twenty four cents a hundred. He bought them by the thousand and dealt them out sparingly.

Some weeks later as I was down the track about a mile, after I shot one grouse, I met Sam Strom coming from Darrington. Together we walked toward home. Suddenly Sam stopped and pointed across the creek to the slope of Toad Mountain.

"See that bear over there? By golly, we're going to have fresh bear meat for supper."

To me it looked too far away, but up went Sam's rifle and he missed. Quickly Sam loaded and shot again as the bear was running. The bear fell over but struggled to get up. Sam fired another shot and missed again. The fourth shot did not miss and the bear lay still.

"I must be getting old," Sam said. "I should not have missed any of those shots. Let's go over and see what we got." Hearing him say "we" made me feel good, as if I had been a party to getting the bear.

We crossed the creek, getting ourselves wet above the knees. That was nothing compared to the excitement of the whole event. The climb up the rocky slope was hard but I looked forward to helping Sam skin the animal. We cleaned out the insides and skinned out a hindquarter.

"That's all we're going to do now," said Sam. "We'll have to have help to carry the rest home. Perhaps your dad will be home by that time."

On the way home I shot another grouse, so now we could have grouse for supper. It was quicker than fixing bear roast. I helped Mama with the birds while Sam told her all that had happened. Soon Papa came home. We had our supper while telling our story all over again.

Pretty soon we started down the track to get the bear. It was still there, although some animal or bird had been trying to eat some of the insides. We cut a pole for a carryall. With the bear's legs tied together and the pole on Papa's and Sam's shoulders we finally got home about dark.

We skinned off the hide and I was given the job of stretching it out on the basement wall to dry. The meat was cut up. Some was given to the Cook family and the Clevelands. The rest was salted down. The liver was not saved — Sam said it was too rich, or something. The bile was saved to be used for burns. I thought about the time I had burned my hand on the exploding firecracker and wished we had had some of the bile instead of Mama's hot water. The bear fat is kind of watery and was saved for greasing our leather boots in order to waterproof them.

Fresh meat was not commonplace, for we had no way of keeping it. Some of the houses on Mercedes street had wooden boxes or cupboards for food, with piped-in water from the creek running over them. That helped some. Food was plentiful but plain, and sometimes it was monotonously the same from day to day. We always had meat of some kind with potatoes, carrots, cabbage, or turnips. For dessert we had home-canned berries, or cooked dried apples, pears, peaches, or apricots. Never was the cake plate or the cooky jar empty at our house. Mama was a good cook, and Ely and I were always hungry, so nothing was ever turned down. A clean plate was the watchword.

Beans were a mainstay. They were served in every way possible, even though they took a long time to cook in that high altitude. Papa built a large box insulated with straw, so a boiling bean kettle could cook a long time without fire. That helped some.

Fresh vegetables were scarce, so the nettle soup and the dandelion greens in the spring were a welcome treat. Someone had told us the tender shoots of ferns were good, but we never liked them. When the kids wanted something special, a bunch of us would hike up to the mines. The cooks were always good to us.

Breakfast was generally oatmeal mush, eggs from our own chickens, ham or bacon, and pancakes. Arbuckle brand coffee was on the stove at all times in case of visitors. There were no cows at Monte so the kids had canned milk mixed with water. As I said before, the coffee grinder going in the morning was the best alarm clock anyone could have. That was the time to eat a big breakfast and start a day of work or play — or misadventure for the kids. One breakfast food I can't forget — the first corn flakes I tasted. They were called Egg-O-See. We didn't like them, especially when someone said they were made of peanut shells. They tasted like them, too.

11

Mischief

As Dan and I were going to our house one day, we saw Ely playing with a puppy. I asked where it came from.

"Papa asked Mr. Kosmoski if we could have one of their puppies," said Ely. "It was brought over a little while ago."

"I'd like to have one of my own," I said. "I wonder if Mr. Kosmoski would let me have one, too. I'm going over now and ask him."

"Sure, I give puppy if you papa say yes," said Kosmoski. "Come tomorrow when you papa say yes."

Sure enough, when my father came home from work, he agreed that each of us could have a dog of our own. Ely's was a white curly-haired poodle and mine was a smooth-haired terrier, black all over. We each liked our own the best and were happy with what we had. I called mine Snap or Snappy and Ely called hers Sport.

I started to train my dog right away. The first thing to teach him was to lead on a leash and the second thing was not to go uptown without the leash. He learned fast, and when I would put my coat on to go out, he would run to where the leash was hanging and beg to go along. One day I decided to test him. I went out and asked Mama to let him out after a little while. I hid behind a bush on the other side of the tracks, and when he came along I ran out waving my arms and yelling. He never tried that again. He was a real smart dog.

The next time I went to the store, Leo remarked that Snap was not such a bad dog even if he was a mongrel. I took that as a compliment.

"Thanks, Leo. I don't suppose you would like to see some of the other tricks I taught him?"

"Sure, I don't have anything better to do," Leo replied.

It wasn't very long before I had shown the way Snap could hang on to a stick, fetch a ball, and shake hands. We were soon tired of playing with the dog. Then I remembered my rifle.

"Say, Leo, I've got a .22 now. Do you want to see it? Sam Strom gave it to me."

"You mean your father let you have a rifle all your own?"

"Yeah. Papa let me have it because I was so careful with the air rifle, and Mr. Strom said I was such a good shot."

"Gosh!" exclaimed Leo. "I don't think my father would let me have anything like this around my sister or the baby."

"Maybe he would let you have one if you were real careful," I said.

"Oh, I'd be careful if I had one. Let me try it," said Leo, running his hands over the barrel.

"O.K. If you're careful. I'll load it outside and you can shoot at that tin can over there."

Leo held the gun straight down and accidentally touched the hair trigger, which I had forgotten to tell him to be careful of. The bullet went through his shoe just missing his big toe. He hopped around wildly.

I finally got him to take his shoe off, and there was no blood, but there *was* a hole right through his shoe and stocking.

"I guess I'm not hurt so bad. I thought I was shot and was afraid to take my shoe off," said Leo. "But what am I going to do about the hole in my shoe? My father will be mad."

"The only thing to do is to tell him what happened," I said. "Blame it on to me for not telling you to be careful about the hair trigger."

I guess Leo must have told his father a good story because a few weeks after that, Leo had a .22 rifle, too. Later Dan Cook and Bert Cleveland had rifles, also. We did not have any more shooting accidents after that. It was a good lesson for all of us.

★   ★   ★

Later that summer a bunch of us boys went up the steep, winding switchback trail to Silver Lake. It is a beautiful lake, surrounded on three sides by steep peaks. It looks as if it could have been an old volcano many years ago. The water is very blue from the melted snows running over the minerals on the sides of the slopes.

The fourth side is like a mountain meadow with heather growing on the gentle slopes, intermingled with low-growing blueberries. They were different than the huckleberries around our house. These were what we had come for. Those delicious sweet blueberries! We filled our pails and ourselves, then wandered over some woods nearby. We found a one-room cabin with the door partly open.

"I wonder who it belongs to," I said. "Let's look inside."

"Better not," said Dan, who was the cautious one. "It must belong to someone and he might come along anytime."

We went in anyway to look around. It was empty except for some shelves on one wall, with some whiskey bottles on them.

"I wonder what's in them," said Bert, and pulled the cork off one of the bottles, then smelled it. "Boy, that stinks." He dropped the bottle on the floor, breaking it. Pretty soon he yelled and hopped around. "It's burning my foot," he cried. "It's burning my foot!"

We got out of the cabin in a hurry and helped Bert to a puddle of water. He got his shoe off and stuck his foot in the water. That helped the hurt. Part of his shoe had been burnt and had a hole in the uppers.

"I'll bet that was an old prospector's cabin," said Dan. "That stuff must have been some acid that is used for testing ores."

Bert was still moaning about his hurt foot, which was red and blistered on top of the instep. "I know my Pa will be mad at me for spoiling my shoe," said Bert, "but I can't hide."

There was nothing we could do but help Bert get down the mountain. He limped badly and we stopped several times to let him soak his foot in a spring or creek. Dan and I felt sorry for him when we left him at his house, but there was nothing else we could do to help. Bert got new shoes later, but I guess they cost him a good spanking.

12

More Mischief

Among other little annoyances for my sister and me, there were problems with our pets. Ely's all-white cat, with a tiger tail, had kittens once in a while and it was Ely's job to give them away, which was not easy. Her dog, Sport, had trouble, too. He had wandered too close to a setting hen and got pecked in the eye. It must have hurt badly because he whimpered a lot. The worst problem was to keep the dog from pawing that hurt eye.

Papa suggested we make some kind of hobble so Sport could not paw his eye. That worked pretty well after we got the right length string so that Sport could still walk but not be able to reach his eye. Sport didn't like to be hobbled, but his eye had a better chance to heal, although he was now blind in that eye. Ely teased me once in a while by saying that now she had a one-eyed brother *and* a one-eyed dog.

I had the biggest problem with my cat. He was an all-tiger cat. He grew to immense size: when fully grown, he weighed eighteen pounds. Like other cats, he wanted to play with the mice or squirrels he caught. He found out that when he played with them in our bathtub, they could not get away because they could not climb out the steep sides. I did not like him to do that, so I separated them when I could. One day when I tried to get them out of the tub, he defied me and I got a bad scratch on my hand. That made me mad. I loaded the .22 and, without thinking, I shot the squirrel right in front of the cat's nose. He flew out of the back door with a screech and I didn't see him for several days. I took the dead squirrel outside and started to clean up the bathtub. It was then I noticed that I had shot a hole in the bottom of the tub. I stood there wondering what I should do. I had not been punished for many of the mischievous things I had done before, but this was the worst I had ever done.

I went to the kitchen where Mama was working. She looked at me and said, "What were you shooting at out there? It sounded like it was in the lean-to."

"That's the trouble, Mama. The cat was playing with a squirrel in the bathtub. When I tried to take it away from him, he scratched me, so I shot the squirrel and it made a hole right through the bottom of the tub. What shall I do?"

"I'll look at it," Mama said. "Maybe we can fix it so it won't leak. Oh, that's not so bad — get a cork and whittle a plug to fit in the hole real tight. But you will have to fix it up with your father yourself."

I fixed the hole so it didn't leak, but still worried about what Papa would say or do. I guess Mama must have covered for me in some way, because I never heard another word about it and later I noticed the hole had been soldered up real good.

I had other problems with my cat. He would fight and sometimes kill the other tomcats in town. Big Pete, the caretaker at the Royal Hotel, was mad. He said my cat killed his tomcats. But he didn't want any female cats because of the trouble of getting rid of the kittens they had.

My cat was gone another time. While I was looking for him uptown, Bert came along and said, "I think I saw him up near Jakey's saloon. Let's go look."

As we came within the lighted circle of the Royal Hotel, with all the tinkling of glass against glass and the laughter of guests, Dan and Joe came out of the shadows. "Elof is looking for his cat," Bert explained.

"Oh, you mean that big tiger cat that fights all the other tomcats?" asked Dan. "I saw him down by Barney's saloon a while ago. It was near one of the cat houses." He snickered a little. "They are closed up now and empty. Let's go down there and look through them."

The invitation was almost irresistible. "My father told me not to go near such places," I said. "I was looking for my cat. Maybe tomorrow."

We got together the next day, and after some arguments about whether we should go to look in one of the huts near the closed-up saloon, we cautiously entered one of the huts whose door was partly open. Everything was there as if the owner was coming right back. Some of the boys picked up some things, but I did not because I did not think I should take other people's things.

When Papa came home that night, he said he had heard that a bunch of boys had gone into some of those houses and that I had been with them.

"Yes, I went with the other boys, but I didn't take anything. I was just curious about what the huts looked like inside."

"I ought to spank you for doing something I had told you not to do, but as long as you didn't take anything I won't do it this time. Let it be a lesson you will remember."

I felt lucky not to get punished. There were other times when I could have been spanked, like when I left tools out where I had used them and let them get rusty, and still other times when I forgot to carry enough water for Mama or didn't split wood or kindling. I was lucky to have good parents and vowed to do better from now on, if I didn't forget.

My big cat sometimes would stay away from home for several days. This time, however, he had been gone for more than a week. I wondered if Big Pete, at the Royal Hotel, had shot him as he had threatened to do on several occasions. As I was searching around the hotel, I saw Big Pete watching me.

"You looking for something?" he asked.

"Yes, I'm looking for my cat. Have you seen him?"

"Yeah, I might have seen that killer cat, then again maybe I haven't. Don't go monkeying around here. You're trespassing. Get out."

"I'm going to look anyhow. I'm not hurting anything."

I found my cat in a berry patch behind the saloon. He had been shot. I knew Big Pete had done it, but there was nothing I could do about it. I took the cat home and buried him under a big rock in back of our house.

I got myself into another problem later that summer. We were all in the kitchen after supper. Suddenly there was a strong smell of skunk. It was so strong that we thought it must come from the lean-to woodshed. No one wanted to go out there to look for fear of getting squirted on. We opened the kitchen door for a while to let the stink out and then went to bed, where the smell was not so bad.

The next morning we saw no skunk, but the smell was still there. During the day, I thought I had a bright idea. I fixed up an old wooden apple box with a sliding door and a figure four trigger and a piece of bacon rind for bait. I showed it to my mother and she said, "What in the world have you got there?"

"I made a trap," I said. "If the skunk comes again, I'm going to try to catch him."

"You had better ask your father about that when he comes home," Mama said. "He may not want you to do that."

I showed the trap to Papa that night and he said, "If it works, what are you going to do with the skunk? Remember, no more stinks."

I set the trap in the woodshed that night. The next morning the trap was sprung and something was stirring inside. Papa said, "You caught something. Maybe a stray cat."

"I hope not. Our two cats and dogs are in the house somewhere, but it might be a stray cat. If it is a skunk, what shall I do with it?"

"That's your problem now," Papa said. After breakfast he went to work, leaving me with the worry. For a while I wished I had not made a trap.

I knew I had to get rid of whatever was in the trap, so very carefully I picked up the box in my arms, hoping not to get squirted on. Carrying it very gently, I crossed the tracks to the creek, lowered it into a pool, and held it down with my foot for several minutes. When I opened the trap door, out floated a dead skunk.

Grabbing it by the tail, I hurried home, very proud, to show Mama and Ely what a good job I had done. I had to show it to the other boys and tell them how I had made the trap, and how lucky I was that I had not gotten squirted. That was the last of the skunks at our house.

13

A Lonely Stranger

Mr. Kosmoski, or Little Pete, as most people called him, was one of the workers at the concentrating mill. He lived in one of the houses down the track from town. He came to our house one evening with some bear meat — he had shot the bear that afternoon. He was all excited, telling in broken English and Russian how the bear had almost got him. He said he shot once, but the bear did not fall down and came flying right at him. His old .38-.55 rifle jammed. By the time he got ready to shoot again the bear was almost upon him. At the second shot the bear was killed. I'll bet it was not funny at the time, but we had a good laugh while he was telling his story with gestures and arms waving.

He had other news, too. It was a little hard to understand him, but we finally figured out that he had sent some money to some friends in a village in Russia, where he came from. He wanted that family to send one of their daughters over here so he could marry her. He didn't know the girl he was getting, but hoped she would be big and strong to help him take care of his house. We thought that was a funny custom, but wished him good luck.

It was several weeks later when Mr. Kosmoski took the noon train out of town. He was all excited, running from one person to another, saying, "I'm going to get my wife in Everett. I'm going to get my wife!" He seemed to be happy, almost dancing in his eagerness to have the train start.

Some days later when the Kosmoskis came back, there was no real opportunity to greet them. Kosmoski hustled his wife away in a big hurry, as if he were ashamed of her. She was crying. Her hair was all awry, her stockings were hanging down around her clodhopper shoes, and her slip was hanging below her dress. She did not look very attractive. We felt sorry for her, for Mama and I could still remember the problems of traveling by boat and train in a strange land and of not knowing the language. Only time would erase the misery of such a trip.

Mama understood the loneliness of a stranger in a new land, so at the first opportunity she went over to visit. They could not understand each other very well, but Mrs. Kosmoski understood that Mama was a sympathetic neighbor even though not the nearest one. The kids in town, however, were not as kind or thoughtful. Whenever she appeared they would run after her shouting, ''You're dirty, you're dirty.'' I regret to say that at times I was among them. She would always say, ''Me clean, me clean,'' and calmly go on her way. She must have had a very unhappy life at Monte Cristo as there were rumors that her husband was mean to her.

I met her many years later in the little town of Robe. She seemed glad to see me. I was embarrassed, thinking of my treatment of her in the past. She was very well dressed and looked very well. She told me she had left Kosmoski and married a very fine man, and she had two children. I was glad she was happy.

14

A Kindly Old Gentleman

Martin Cummins was a part-time prospector who lived down the river from town, near the Kosmoskis and the section boss. He made a lot of diggings and prospect holes in many places around Monte. As soon as he found a little gold in any of these diggings, he would sell the claim for a case of whiskey or a grubstake in order to hunt up some more prospects and go through the same deal again. I have seen him many times stumbling down the street, teetering on his toes to keep his balance, with a big smile and a wave of hands as he passed other people. He was a good-natured man, drunk or sober.

He was a hard worker, however, as anyone who has ever hunted for minerals would know. Drilling holes by hand and building shelters of logs or lumber carried up the mountains on your back is not easy work. He enjoyed the mountains and he had the same hopes that all prospectors have, of some day finding something really big.

Martin, as he liked to be called, also was nicknamed XYZ, and The Duke of Monte Cristo. It has been said that many of his mining claims were recorded with those names. He was a very good friend of my father, and he helped us locate some claims of our own. They were on Cadet Peak and were named The Ely, the Elof, and the Good Hope. They "showed" very good in spots when they were smelted during assay. One picked-out sample assayed seventy-six dollars a ton gold, which is very high. My father never had the money to develop them, to do the necessary assessment work, or to patent them, and so they reverted to the government.

At Christmas time Mr. Vogelsburg, the surveyor, and his wife came to visit and have a little liquid refreshments. Mr. and Mrs. Cleveland and Mr. and Mrs. Kyes also came. The Cook family did not come then as they did not drink, so they came at another time for coffee and cake and to look at our tree, decorated with colored strings of paper and red apples from the store, and miners' candles.

In the early evening, it was starting to snow very heavily, and our visitors were about to leave when there came a knock on the door. There stood Martin Cummins. "Can I come in and stay for the night, Otto?" he said. "I've been drinking a little and I'm afraid I might fall in the creek."

Papa didn't like for him to stay, but the cabin was close to the creek and the snow was getting worse, so he said, "O.K., Martin, you had better stay until the weather gets better."

The other people left and Papa sat Martin in a big rocking chair with a quilt wrapped around him, then said, "Well, Martin, I see you found a Christmas bottle. It is just as well you didn't try to get home. Crossing that railroad bridge is not so good with all the snow on it."

Papa wasn't sure if Martin heard him, because Martin said, "Those were the days. Did I ever tell you about the time I found a hundred pounds of gold?"

Papa said, "There were never any such days. You're dreaming."

But Martin didn't hear him. "I had been panning all day in a stream in California," Martin continued. "I straightened my aching back and glanced up at the hill above me and saw a gleaming. I went to it and knew that it was gold!" Martin stood up unsteadily in his excitement, then sank back in the chair.

Papa stoked up the potbellied stove with some powdery coal he had scrounged from the roundhouse, and we all went to bed.

We had not been in bed long before there was a loud explosion in the living room. We jumped out of bed to find the living room full of smoke, the stove on its side, and the floor covered with fire and ashes.

Our first thought was to put out the fire on the floor. Papa got some water from the kitchen and that put the fire out, but it made more soot and steam. It was a mess. We were lucky the house did not burn down. It would have been bad to have no home or furniture on a freezing winter night.

Still in our nightshirts, we opened the doors and windows to let out the smoke, then we dressed in the cold with some warm clothing, put up the stove, and got a fire started again. Papa looked around and said, "Well, this is a mess, but we are lucky that the house did not burn. This dirt can be cleaned up."

Mama did not feel the same way. She had so enjoyed the new wallpaper that had just been put up before the holidays and now it was a dirty, sooty mess.

Suddenly someone said, "Where's Martin?" We found him in the farthest corner with the quilt and rocking chair on top of him. He was not hurt, just a little scared and a good deal more sober. "What happened?" he wondered.

Papa said, "I guess I must have forgotten to open the damper when I stoked up the stove with the fine coal."

We all stood and looked at each other and at the dirty mess, shivering a little for the room was not too warm yet. Martin said, "I think I'll go home now. It's not snowing so much and I feel better." And away he went. I guess he thought he would be safer there. There was no more to be done then, so we went to bed to try to sleep in the rooms smelling of soot.

The next day, the day after Christmas, Papa went back to work. The rest of us stayed home to clean up things. Mama was on her knees scrubbing the floor, while Ely and I were washing the woodwork and windows, when there was a knock on the door. There stood Martin.

"I left you in an awful mess last night. I've come to help." He looked at Mama, scrubbing away with tears in her eyes because the new wallpaper had been ruined, then said, "Lady, let me do that. I feel partly responsible for the whole thing. Go in the kitchen and we will soon have it all cleaned up."

When we got through with the floor, the windows, and the wood-work, it didn't look too bad. Mama came in to see and still complained about what had happened to the new flowery wallpaper which she had admired so much.

Martin said, "I think I can fix that. I'll go uptown, but will be back in a little while." And away he went.

He came back in a little while with a large bundle of newspapers. He must have scrounged a lot of places to have been able to get so many. Newspapers were scarce in Monte. We wondered what he was going to do with them until he said, "Mrs. Norman, if you will mix up some flour and water we will paste these newspapers on the walls and ceiling. That will be a good clean foundation for some wallpaper later on."

We all got busy. Mama made the paste and I smeared paper while Martin slapped it on the walls. The ceilings were the worst. When we were through it was a crazy mixture of reading material, some upside down and some sideways, but everything was clean and did not smell of smoke and dirt.

When Papa came home he was surprised to see how clean every-thing was and said, "You all did a good job. I'll have to invite Martin over to have a drink or two for the work he did, and Petra, some day we will get some real wallpaper that you will like just as much as the other."

Several weeks later there was an express package for us. We had not ordered anything, so we were surprised to find some new wallpaper. Martin came over the next day and admitted that he had ordered it because he thought he had been the main reason for the stove explo-sion.

"I want to come over Sunday to help put it on. There is a different pattern for the ceiling and some border, too."

Sunday was a busy day. I again pasted and Papa and Martin were kept busy. When we were all done, even Mama had to admit that she liked it better than what had been on there before.

I became better acquainted with Mr. Cummins the next spring. He had been careless in going out in the bright sunlight shining on the snow, without darkening the glare by putting sooty rings around his eyes. He became snowblind, which was very painful, with matter oozing from the eyes.

Somehow it became my job to go to Martin's cabin every morning before school to bring him something to eat or cook breakfast, and to bathe his eyes. Also, I went after school to get wood for the fire and get him something to eat. He complained at times that my cooking was not as good as my mother's or even his own. I guess he liked his own meals pretty well — he certainly had had lots of cooking practice in all those years of being a bachelor.

When the pain became too bad I would give him a teaspoon of laudanum to ease it. My father told me to be careful and not give it to Martin if he had been drinking. I was also told to take Martin's gun away if I could find it, which I did.

I suppose it was lonesome to be blind and alone because he became very confidential while laid up, and told me things of his past that he might not have told me otherwise. He said he was the youngest son of a very rich family in Ireland and had been a teacher in a university there. Drinking was his downfall.

He said that he embarrassed his family, so they sent him to America with the understanding that he should stay away, and that he would receive a certain amount of money if he did so. "For a while I did so," he said. "But that is all in the past. I am all on my own now. I am no longer a remittance man."

I enjoyed those trips to his cabin as the days went on. He told me about his many prospecting hikes, and how to spot claims, and of finding gold deposits. I reminded him of the time he had said he found a hundred pounds of gold. He chuckled and said, "No, that was just a miner's dream. If I had I probably would be drunk yet."

Later, when he got better he told me to bring his gun back. He said, "I am glad you took it. I might have been tempted to use it when I thought I was going to be blind forever."

Old XYZ was quite a guy when you got to know him as I did, drunk or sober. Just a kindly old gentleman who liked to drink.

15

The Exception To Our Good Record

Mining has always been hazardous for the miners, mostly because of falling rock or mishandled caps or dynamite. There was no doctor in the tiny community, but everyone had some kind of salve and patent medicine at home. Whiskey was used in many cases as a sedative, even for toothaches, which I had plenty of. Mr. Kyes was a big help, too. His store had laudanum, paregoric, and opium pills, which were used in extreme cases.

Most bad accidents were taken care of at Mrs. Kimball's house because, as I said earlier, she had been a nurse. The patients seemed to get along quite well, thanks to her care.

In one serious accident at the Mystery mine, four miners were killed. No one knew what had caused the tremendous explosion. The bodies were so badly mangled that no one could tell which person was which. Four coffins came up from Everett and four names were placed on them before they were sent away to some cemetery for burial.

Orville Kimball was hurt at the same time. He was visiting his father, who was foreman at the mine. Orville was standing at the entrance of the mine when the explosion occurred. The concussion tossed him across the room and broke his eardrums. He had a bad time at school after that because he could not hear. The Kimballs moved away soon after that, so Orville could go to a special school.

I have often wondered about the fact that not one of the boys at Monte Cristo had any shooting accidents, except that one time when Leo shot a hole in his shoe with my .22. We must have been well instructed by our fathers. I don't think I would trust too many ten- or eleven-year-old youngsters with rifles all by themselves.

There was, however, one exception to our good record. A small boy, about seven or eight, came with his family to visit the mine owners. When he saw the rifles the other boys had, he begged for one, too. When the boy visited the Golden Cord mine, the camp cook made friends with him and pretended to take the gun away from him. With the cook pulling on the barrel of the gun and the boy tugging on the stock, the rifle suddenly fired. The bullet hit the cook in the stomach.

The little boy cried hard and threw the .22 down the mountain. The cook, though badly wounded and in great pain, kept repeating, "Don't blame the boy. It was my fault. Don't blame the boy." A makeshift stretcher was made of a blanket and two poles to carry the wounded man down the trail to town. In the meantime, someone had run to Kyes' store in town and Jim came up with paregoric and opium pills to ease the pain. But nothing could be done to save the man's life. He died on the way down the track on the speeding push car. His only thoughts were of the boy. Over and over he kept repeating, "Don't blame the boy, don't blame the boy."

The accident had a sobering effect on the folks at Monte. Our rifles were taken away from us for the rest of that summer, even though we had had no mishaps among us and had nothing to do with the shooting. We had to go back to our air rifles and some homemade slingshots.

16

The Train Crews

The following winter was very bad. Lots of snow fell all over the Northwest. The trains were not coming to town regularly. They came only when the rotary plows could be spared from other tracks and when the ore cars had to be hauled away.

The schoolteacher we had at that time had promised to go home to her folks for Christmas. When the train did not come up to Monte before the holidays, she insisted on tramping the fourteen miles to Silverton. The weather was not fit for traveling, but nothing could change her mind; nor would she even change from her skirts into a pair of pants. Luckily the phone lines were not down and when she did not arrive in Silverton by a certain time, a rescue team of three men and a horse went after her.

They found her about halfway down to Silverton, lying exhausted in the snow. She was lucky such a determined group of men found her before she froze. They had had an arduous trip, breaking trail for themselves and the horse.

When she refused to mount the horse astraddle, one of the exasperated miners yelled at the stubborn female, "Get on that d--n horse. I've seen a woman's legs before."

They got her to Silverton where she later caught the train home. The men came back the next day with a story to tell. The teacher did not return to Monte, so the kids had a long vacation before another teacher came.

It continued to snow. Before the winter ended, sixteen feet had fallen. Huge slides tumbled down the mountains, taking trees and boulders with them and covering tracks many feet deep in spots. In one such slide the rotary plow hit a huge rock, damaging the plow. Repairs had to be made on the spot as snow had piled up behind the train and other rotaries were too busy elsewhere to be spared for clearing here. Blasting had to be done to clear away the rocks and trees carried by the slide. The hundred Japanese men in the work crew they had with the train did a lot of snow shoveling while the repairs were being made. After the slide had been cleared, the train continued to the half mile switchback, which also had to be shoveled out by hand. During this delay the food on the train ran out, and the train crew with the hundred Japanese men tramped to Monte for meals, and sometimes slept there whenever they could find shelter in someone's home.

We all worked hard to feed all these men, as did others. Most of the work fell on the mothers in town and I know my mother did her share. Meals were constantly being prepared and served, and we had no privacy with men sleeping in shifts on our living room floor. After a week of feeding extra people, the food in town was running low. All we had left in our house were beans and dried codfish.

Sam Strom was staying at our house. He told Papa that he thought he knew of some deer that had been marooned by the sudden and heavy snows. He said they might not still be there or might even be dead, but if Papa would go with him, he thought it was worthwhile to try to find them. They went down the tracks to near Weedin Falls and spotted two deer — half starved, skinny little things, but they helped some in the food situation.

When the repairs were made and the train finally reached Monte, its troubles were not over. The snow had broken down the turntable housing. All the large timbering had to be cleared away and the turntable pit shoveled out. The rotary and the engine were able to get turned around for the trip back to civilization, with large orders for supplies, mostly paid for by checks from the railway company.

In the meantime the mines had closed down, not because of the snow, but because the concentrator had filled up all the ore cars and had no train to take them away. The trains kept a fairly consistent schedule the rest of the winter. The Japanese section crew, however, were kept busy shoveling out the turntable until a covering building was constructed over it the next spring.

With all the broken timbers from the crushed building, I did not have to help cut down any trees for firewood. I did, however, blast down one tree with dynamite, just to see how it would work. I did not do that again. First it was a big job to bore the hole for the dynamite, and then the tree fell the wrong way. There was some rivalry among the people about who was getting the best lumber from the turntable. I suppose the Norman family got the most because we were closer. We all had plenty of work to do besides the regular chores.

★ ★ ★

The permanent Japanese section crew always had an Irish section boss. Their job was to keep the track in good repair for seven miles, or half the distance to Silverton. They were kept busy removing rolled down rocks, replacing rotted ties, straightening rails, as well as reporting any job too big for seven or eight men to handle, such as replacing rock rip-rap between the track and the river.

These crews were changed once in a while. The same boss always went with the same crew. The boss selected one man to keep house for him on a part-time basis. This sometimes created a problem, because that man would at times be snug in the house doing washing, ironing, or cooking, while the others were outside in bad weather.

My sister and I got along fairly well with the Japanese, probably because we lived much closer to them than the other townspeople.

I went to their one-room house quite often. It was across a small gully from our home. Their house was not too well kept up, and their two-tiered bunks were not always made up. However, they kept their bodies and clothing clean in the attached steam room, where they had a stove going and a big iron kettle of water. It was an every evening ritual for them to take a steam bath and shower.

They all smoked Bull Durham cigarettes, but also smoked something in the house that smelled odd. I found out later that it was opium. Rice was one of their main foods. It must have had the husks on, because they rubbed the rice briskly between their hands while squatting in the creek.

One of their foods came in little tubs with Japanese writing on it. These tubs contained small two-inch fish, something like our porgies. These they ate raw — heads, tails, and all. This was supposed to be a delicacy. These little fish floated in a thick molasses-like sauce which the men drank hot. All this was a special treat for them and on occasion they would offer me some, but I always refused.

Once in a while I gave them some cookies or a piece of cake, or a loaf of homemade bread. These gifts were accepted with low bows accompanied with sharp inward breaths, causing hissing sounds. This sound was supposed to show the greatest pleasure and politeness.

One winter evening we heard loud noises from the Japanese house. Soon after, there was a loud banging on our door. Papa opened it and there stood one of the section men gasping for breath. He kept pointing down toward his house and we saw other Japanese men shouting at us. We let him in and Papa told me to get his .32-.40 rifle, which he fired into the air. The other men turned back.

The Japanese was still fighting for air and picking at his neck. On looking closer, we found a wire loop deep around his neck buried in the flesh.

"No wonder he's fighting for air," Papa said. "Get my wire cutters, Elof, I think I can cut the wire rather than trying to untwist the loop."

The man moaned when Papa dug deep to cut the wire, but grinned with relief when he could breathe freely again. Papa got some cloth to stop the bleeding. Afterward we had some tea and tried to find out what the trouble was. We never did find out why the other Japanese were after him. His English was so poor we didn't get sense out of what he was trying to tell us.

He did not want to go to bed, but sat in the living room, very much afraid the other men might come after him. None of us slept very much that night. I think that my friendship with the whole section crew kept them from doing us any harm.

The next morning we sneaked him aboard the caboose of the ore train, which left right away. The other Japanese did not show up at all. They were taken away on the noon train without any trouble. A new section crew who seemed to be more agreeable came in a few days, and everything went on as usual.

Mama, Mrs. Otto Norman
Elof Norman
Ely Norman 1902

Papa, Otto Norman 1915

Cook family children,
Monte Cristo, 1902.
Dan (the oldest),
Joe, Claud, Elsworth,
Grace, Belle, and Ethel

Our stepmother,
Ely, and Papa, 1917

Jim Kyes with his famous
.35 caliber Winchester rifle.
Monte Cristo, 1903.
Terminal building
in background.

Miss Rice
Schoolteacher at
Monte Cristo, 1906-1907

"Black Jack"
Foreman at Mystery Mine,
Monte Cristo, 1902-1907

Dedication and memorial service for James E. Kyes. His widow, his mother, his brother-in-law, and his nephew, Monte Cristo, 1962

Joe Cook, Mrs. Weeks (Miss Rice), and Ely (now Mrs. Bridgham). Monte Cristo, 1972

Joe Cook (standing), Mrs. Bridgham, Mrs. Weeks, Elof Norman Monte Cristo, 1974

17

The Carefree Life

Mr. Makintosh, or McIntosh, or MacIntosh (I have never seen it spelled) was another good friend of my father. He was caretaker of the Penn Mining Company's holdings at Goat Lake, across the mountains north of Monte Cristo. These mines were not being worked at this time. He also had a cabin at Barlow Pass near the tracks, so the train could drop off his supplies. From there he packed them up the trail to Goat Lake. His house there was part of the former bunk house, which he had partitioned off. He was very neat in regard to himself and his home. Everything was put in its place and no one was allowed to touch or disturb any of the furniture. He was very conscious of the danger of becoming snowblind, and he had everything arranged so he could move about, if blind, and get himself something to eat if nothing had been disturbed.

His only company were numerous cats. He often said, "The more the merrier." He had them well trained, too. They did not get in his way when he did any work around the house. He had cut several openings in the outside wall, with shutters hinged at the top. Little openings for the small cats and large openings for the big ones. When Mackintosh said "Scat," the cats flew for the openings in a scramble to get away. It was amusing to watch them scramble amid a bumping of heads against the shutters and the clatter of the swinging shutters. Mackintosh smiled whenever one of them stuck its head in to see if it was safe to come back.

My father and I visited him as often as we could. We were much interested in the future development of that property. The ore vein there had a good showing, but transportation and financing were the big problems. The only way to get ore out was by a narrow and sometimes steep trail. The owners were trying to raise money to tunnel through the mountain to Monte Cristo and rail transportation, but were not successful. The big financiers were not interested. They still remembered Mr. Rockefeller and his losses at Monte, and did not want anything to do with the place.

It is regretful that my father did not patent our claims (The Ely, The Elof, and The Good Hope, which I mentioned earlier), which was possible at that time. I suppose that money was the main reason that was not done nor the claim developed. I am like many other people, who believe that with modern equipment and better transportation, the ores at Monte can be taken out at a profit, although ecology seems to be more important nowadays than profit from industry. Only the future holds the answer.

★ ★ ★

Fortunate were the children who had the experience of living the carefree life we had at Monte Cristo. Climbing mountains, going fishing, and hunting grouse with my .22; even picking the huckleberries and wild blackberries was not a chore when a group of us went together. Naturally, we had our chores to do around the house, like carrying water from the downstairs pump (which had to be thawed out in the winter), keeping the wood box filled, and keeping the snow shoveled off the outside stairway and the walkway. The grown folks worked long hours at hard labor, but for the children it was the most joyous and healthful experience. No one could have a better growing-up time than we did.

With all my mischief and escapades, I received only one spanking, though very likely I deserved others. That spanking came because of a misunderstanding. My father did not write very good English, so it was my job to write our grocery orders to Bruhn and Henry's mercantile store in Snohomish, where supplies were cheaper than at Kyes' store. These orders always went out on the noon train.

On this particular day I brought my lunch to school with me and was not going home for a hot lunch. Papa went by the school while I was playing outside. He waved for me to come with him. I yelled back and said that I had a sandwich with me and kept on playing.

When I got home after school, my mother said, "Elof, you're in trouble. Your papa is real mad at you because you didn't come home with him at lunchtime."

"But, Mama," I said. "I hollered and told Papa that I had my lunch with me."

"He didn't want you to come home to eat," she said. "He wanted you to write an order to Bruhn and Henry to go out on the train that was waiting. He was still pretty mad when he went to work."

When Papa got home from work, I got a real spanking. It didn't hurt so much when I noticed tears in *his* eyes. He told me later that he should have had me write out the order the evening before, instead of waiting until the next day, but he said that I should have come with him when he asked me to come. Thinking back, I guess we were pretty good pals. I wonder, too, if I wasn't a spoiled brat at times: my being the third child born but the first one to live might have made some difference in my father's attitude toward me and his indulgence in regard to some of my misbehavior.

The children at Monte could always find plenty of things to do to enjoy themselves. Entertainment for the grown folks was not so easy to come by. The dance pavilion had dances occasionally, with music brought in from somewhere. The dances seemed to be for the mine owners and foremen and their wives, although the saloon keepers came and brought some of their "ladies." The wives did not socialize with them. The common miners were never invited to these parties and had to find their recreation elsewhere. My sister and I had been told not to go near the place when there was a dance going on, but we sneaked over to listen to the music and watch the dancing.

The Royal Hotel had a Victrola on the back bar. Sometimes Mrs. Sheedy would let the kids stand in the doorway to listen to it playing. Ely was a little frightened of it because someone had told her that there was a little man inside of the box who did all the singing, and she thought he might come out and chase her. We had fun teasing her. No dancing was allowed in the saloons, but some singing went on, especially when someone pounded on the piano in Barney's saloon. Drinking and gambling were the main forms of entertainment for the miners.

Papa had an accordion and played some old Scandinavian tunes. Martin Cummins brought his fiddle at times and played Irish jigs. When the two got together it was some conglomeration of noises. They seemed to enjoy it, with the tapping of feet and smiling at each other and at Ely's and my antics as we tried to imitate the dancers we had seen at the pavilion.

Once in a while a poker party got started at our house, with our two boarders and some other workers. They played for money, but only for pennies, nickels, and dimes, so I guess it was more for pastime than anything else. Drinking was part of the entertainment and it became my job to beat the eggs by hand for eggnog. This, mixed with whiskey or rum, made the party a little merrier. Papa was careful not to let me have much, although I got a sip once in a while for my labors.

Recreation was not the most important part of life at Monte Cristo. After working ten or twelve hours a day, six days a week, rest was more necessary for the people there.

18

The Iron Wheels Turned Relentlessly

In 1906 there was a slight depression at Monte. The Philo mine had shut down some time ago. The Comet mine tried to run, but only a little high-grading was being done by Mackinaw Johnson and the Cowden boy. They blasted in the tunnel and picked out the richer pieces of ore, and backpacked those down the mountain to a bunker near the depot until they had enough for shipping to the smelter.

Only a few men were working at the Mystery and the Pride mines. The only mines running steadily were the Golden Cord, the Justice, and the Rainey mine when they could get the water pumped out.

At the request of the mine owners, a survey was made by Mr. Vogelsburg, the surveyor, to determine where a certain vein of ore might be found lower down the mountain. Because of the broken rock formations, this was something of a gamble. However, according to the prevailing faults, a spot was decided on to start drilling. On this job a crew of men agreed to work for wages half in cash and half in scrip. The drilling went on for three months. Then the owners ran short of money, and all work stopped. During this time the other mines had also lost their veins of ore, so the concentrator mill closed, too.

The scrip, which was issued by the mine owners, looked like a check, but it was actually a promissory note which could only be redeemed by the signer when he had the money. Some of the stores in Everett and Seattle refused to cash the scrip, but the saloons would give fifty percent of value. Naturally the miners cashed the scrip first because no one knew if it would ever be redeemed at full value. It was reported later that the scrip was redeemed at eight cents on the dollar.

During this time some of the families were moving away. The Kimballs and the Clevelands had left a few weeks ago. The Kyes and Cook families were preparing to go soon. The day they left I felt deserted and alone. I had watched them loading their furniture aboard the boxcars the day before, and wondered what would happen when Papa had no more work.

"Do you understand what is happening here?" Papa said.

"I understand only one thing," I replied. "My friends are leaving. I suppose we will have to go too someday."

"Yes, Elof," Papa said. "Unless more of the mines start up again we will have to move. I would not like to leave our home which we have all enjoyed."

The work continued at a reduced scale that summer. With the mines operating only part-time, the concentrator ran only once in a while. The trains came only when they had ore cars to take away. Most of the miners were already gone.

As the work slowed up, more miners moved away. Mrs. Sheedy and Mr. Cohen closed up the hotel, leaving Big Pete as caretaker. Mr. Hickey also lost his job and moved away with his two girls.

Miss Rice, our schoolteacher, had to move, so her mother came up to keep house for her at a small house near the old hotel. Some snow fell but not enough to hinder what little work was going on. Although Mr. and Mrs. Kyes had moved away with their children, Mr. Kyes came back to take care of his store and work in his claim, the Mackinaw mine, which was his biggest interest.

Mrs. Cook had always disliked Monte Cristo. She confessed to having a closed-in feeling from the high peaks all around the little valley. Now that everything seemed to be closing down, she persuaded Mr. Cook to move away, although he still had a job there. Mr. Cook came back with Dan and Joe after the rest of the family had been settled elsewhere. He ran the donkey engine for the Rainey mine.

It was with mixed feelings that I watched the Cooks and the Kyes board the train. "All aboard, all aboard," shouted the conductor, waving his arms. Ever so slightly the train started to move as Mr. Resigue opened the throttle. The iron wheels turned relentlessly, taking the families away from Monte. It was a lonely feeling for us who were left wondering what was in store for us in the future.

With less and less ore the trains came only occasionally, and with winter coming on, Miss Rice's mother thought she had better go back home, rather than get snowed in for the winter. So Miss Rice came to stay at our house. Mama was glad for the companionship and the help she got in the kitchen from Miss Rice.

With fewer children in school, Miss Rice had quite a time keeping us busy, without giving us too long a lesson. To fill in the time she taught drawing, sewing, clay modeling and raffia weaving for baskets. Her wages were $60.00 a month, out of which she paid $25.00 a month room and board.

Joe Cook twisted his knee while sliding. He had had problems with that knee ever since he had hurt it on the turntable, so his father took the two boys down to Lake Stevens where the rest of the family were living. But he came back to his job as engineer at the Rainey mine.

One family did move to Monte Cristo that late fall, otherwise only Ely and I would have been going to school. This family had four children. (I do not remember their name.) Three were of school age and one daughter had consumption. They came only for this daughter's health. However, she did not get any better and they moved away in the spring. She died shortly afterwards. Now only Ely and I were in school.

The work at the mines progressed at a slower and slower pace. The train came up only once in a while to take away the full ore cars. Everyone knew that the end of mining at Monte was in sight. We all wondered what we were going to do when all the mining stopped, and where we would be, as the prospects for continued work did not look too good.

Miss Rice left at the end of the school term, and did not come back to Monte the following year, even though there would be school for any children remaining there. She had other commitments to teach elsewhere. It was a sad time for all of us to see her go.

All the properties at Monte Cristo went into receivership that summer (1906). Papa was lucky. He and Mr. Vogelsburg were hired as watchmen or caretakers for the properties. Their pay was $75.00 a month each. They did not have to punch a clock or keep regular hours. It was the easiest time that my father ever had. His hardest work during the winter was shoveling the snow off the three roof levels of the concentrator — at times the snow fell two feet overnight. I helped with this, too. Otherwise, the time was his own. There would have been plenty of vandalism if no one had been there to prevent destruction by occasional tourists. We were lucky to be able to stay in our home.

The only people left at Monte were Jim Kyes, who still had great hopes for his mine near the Weedin Creek Falls; Big Pete, the caretaker at the Royal Hotel; Mr. and Mrs. Vogelsburg; and the Norman family of four. Mackinaw Johnson and the Cowden boy, Harry, came in the summer to high-grade at the Comet mine or to do assessment work. Occasionally some curious tourists or climbers would show up with all kinds of questions about where to pan some gold. They did not seem to understand that there was no panning of gold at Monte, only hard rock mining.

Now that the trains were running only as far as Silverton, our biggest problem was to have enough food for the winter. Some foods had been left at the mines when they shut down, and we helped ourselves to hams, bacon, beans, rice, and other nonperishable foods. This saved us having to make some of those trips of 14 miles to Silverton and back with a loaded packsack. Papa shot an immense goat in the late fall. The weather was cool enough so we did not have to salt it down or can any of it, and we had fresh meat for a long time. We sold the hide later to a saloon keeper in Seattle who had the whole animal stuffed and then mounted it on a shelf above the back bar.

On the numerous trips we made to Silverton, I always went along and carried a small pack, too. My .22 went along as far as Barlow Pass, where I ditched it under Mr. Mackintosh's cabin until the return trip. I generally was able to shoot a grouse between Barlow and home. Papa carried fifty or sixty pounds and I had about fifteen pounds. My father would plod, plod the entire way home with a loaded pack, without stopping, but I would get impatient and go fast for a couple of miles, then rest up against a bank until he came along. That was the usual routine on each trip.

19

"Very Little Pain"

I had a lot of toothaches that summer. When it hurt real bad, Papa would let me hold a little whiskey in my mouth, with a caution not to swallow it. That helped some but was not a cure. I also had trouble with my one good eye.

Papa said, "Something has to be done for your eye, Elof. The only thing to do is to go to a doctor in Seattle. We'll have a dentist fix your teeth at the same time."

I didn't care too much about going to a dentist, but when I thought about how the teeth hurt, the dentist couldn't be much worse.

We walked to Silverton the next day. The trains were coming up intermittently, so we stayed at the Hickey home for two days until the train came to take us to Everett.

Papa asked me if I would like to live in a city. I looked around at all the people and the stores. It was exciting and different, but there was no grouse hunting and all the people were strangers. I said, "I guess I wouldn't like to right now."

"This is where you will live if you go to high school," Papa said. "But I am glad you are content with your mother and me for the present."

We walked down to the docks to watch for the boat for Seattle. (I still don't know why we did not go to a doctor in Everett.) The waterfront seemed to be the poorer part of town, as the people were not dressed up like they were uptown.

The water was calm, but I was not sure I would like the trip on the boat. I still remembered the steerage trip on Oscar II from Denmark. Papa said it would be a pleasant trip. Across the bay we could see some tall mountains with snow on them. Papa said they were the Olympics and that the peaks were 10,000 feet high.

Soon the boat came and some people got off. The captain took tickets and we went on. I watched the coastline as the boat steamed toward Seattle, and I wished Mama and Ely could have been along. Papa pointed out the different places of interest. To the west were Hat Island and Whidbey Island, to the east the irregular coast of the mainland, with its little settlements south of Everett. First Mukilteo, then Edmonds and Ballard and the skyline of Seattle.

When the boat docked, we found a little hotel to stay at. I was so quiet that Papa said, "Don't worry about the dentist. It won't be bad at all."

We found a doctor on Pike Street. After looking at my eye he said my trouble was conjunctivitis. He put some drops in my eye and gave us a prescription for some salve, so we could do our own doctoring at Monte.

My eye was much better the next morning, so we looked up a dentist. As Jim Kyes would have said, "That was a horse of a different color." I was scared when the dentist sat me in the chair and began to probe with a pick and a mirror. "What do you find?" I asked.

"Well, I'll get along better if you don't try to talk. Some will have to be pulled and several will have big fillings. They must have been hurting you for some time."

The work started and everything was a blur, partly from the pain and partly from the anesthetic, which did not help much. I was glad when the dentist quit for the day. There was more work to be done the next day, but the worst was over. The dentist had said, "Very little pain." I guess he must have meant to him, because I felt enough. I was glad, however, that I had no more toothache; at least that was something to give thanks for, until some other teeth went bad.

"Before we go home," Papa said, "I want to show you something. That goat I shot last year has been stuffed and mounted by a saloon keeper to display in his saloon. I think I know where the place is."

He took me to a basement saloon called Billy-De-Mug's place on Pioneer Square. The bartender did not want to let me come in until Papa told him he wanted to show me the big goat mounted above the back bar. The goat looked huge and very natural mounted above the mirrored bar. The bartender said that people came from all over Seattle to see the biggest goat ever seen. He was surprised when Papa told him he had shot it at Monte Cristo last year. He didn't think there was anyone living up there any more, so we told him there were about a dozen people there now.

The big goat was not the only reason people came to Billy-De-Mug's. He served the biggest mug of beer in Seattle (16 ounces) for a nickel. With the offer of free lunch with a glass of beer, the place was crowded. One man was busy trying to keep out the free loaders. He wasn't completely successful, however, because I saw several men hand their glasses to their pals so they, too, could get in line for the free lunch. Papa had a beer and some lunch, too, and slipped me a sandwich. He did not drink all of the beer, but soon had found someone to take his half-emptied glass.

We took the boat to Everett the next day. The train had already left, so we had to wait several days at a hotel before we could get to Silverton. Papa did a little shopping but would not tell what he bought, although I knew it was some kind of presents.

Arriving in Silverton, we bought some food supplies and then started walking to Monte. We were glad to be home again. Mama had to look at my eye and my teeth to see what the doctors had done. Then Papa brought out the packages he had bought in Everett. In one was a pair of shoes for Mama, a little too fancy for hiking, I thought; but Mama liked them. In the other package was a doll for Ely. That was the first boughten doll she had ever received.

20

The Awfulest Messes

The watchman's job did not keep my father very busy. The usual work of falling trees and cutting them up for firewood was soon done, and the basement was full. The berry picking and the canning were finished, too. That left us with a lot of spare time for hunting and fishing in the nearby Weedin Creek and the more distant Palmer Creek.

Neither the Glacier nor the 76 Creeks at Monte had any fish in them due to the earlier pollution by the concentrator mill. Nor did the Sauk River where these two creeks joined. We had never tried to fish the Sauk because of the arsenic pollution.

One day my father said he wanted to try some fishing on the Sauk River farther away, where it flowed toward Darrington. Papa and I fished a little before we came to Barlow Pass, but had no luck. We tried again after leaving the tracks and went along the old tote road where it followed the river. We had good luck and continued on to where Elliot Creek comes down from Goat Lake.

There we made camp and built a crude lean-to shelter out of some discarded split cedar shakes, so we could sleep dry in case of rain or heavy dew. Papa built the fire while I cleaned some fish. The smell of bacon and trout and coffee made us more hungry than we thought we were. After cleaning up the tin dishes and frying pan, we rolled up in our Hudson Bay blankets and were soon asleep.

The next couple of days we caught plenty of fish. We kept the cleaned trout in a weighted gunny sack in a pool in the river to keep them fresh. We had seen a few salmon while fishing, but they were pretty badly beaten up in their struggles upstream. Papa thought we might be able to get some fresher ones further downstream where the water was deeper.

The next day we fished downstream several miles away from our camp and within a mile of the Bedal family home. The Bedals lived on a 160 acre homestead. Mr. Bedal was French and Mrs. Bedal was Indian, and they had five children. They made their living by hand-logging shingle bolts and floating them down the Sauk to a mill in Darrington.

We caught plenty of trout, but had not seen any good salmon. It was late afternoon and the weather threatened rain. Papa said, "We had better hurry back to camp before we get wet."

"I would rather go to the Bedals' home now that we are so close," I said.

"No, I don't want to leave the camp alone overnight," Papa said. "A bear might ruin the camp looking for food, or even a skunk might come. We had better hurry."

It started to rain real hard. The wind blew so hard that tree branches came off, but luckily none hit us. We were soon soaked. Papa said, "I guess I was wrong. We should have gone to the Bedals' after all. Our camp wouldn't give us much shelter in this kind of storm. If I remember right there is a man living up on the hillside away from the river. If I can find the side trail we can be at his house in a little while."

It was very dark now, but Papa found the trail. We went along it for a ways, but it was so narrow and the woods were so dark that we soon lost it. Papa stopped, with me hanging on to his coat tail and wondering what we should do. "I'm afraid to go down to the tote road," he said. "It's too close to the river and we might fall in and never get out of it in the dark. We had better stay up here in the woods and work our way back toward the Bedals' place, where we should have gone in the first place."

It was now so dark that we could not see a thing. Papa kept bumping into trees and stumbling over roots and snags. I sheltered myself somewhat by hanging on to his coat tail and ducking my head behind his back. When Papa fell down a gully, I fell, too. The only light we got was from an occasional flash of lightning. It became cold, too. I was beginning to tire and was afraid, wondering how it was all going to end. Several times we fell down gullies into patches of devil's club and the thorns stuck in our hands and faces. Falling down slopes and climbing up the other side, bumping into trees, finally played me out. It seemed to me that we had been struggling for hours.

Papa carried me on his back for a while, but that made it worse for him. He stumbled onto a huge fallen tree. I was asleep part of the time, completely exhausted. Papa laid me in a little hollow between the uprooted tree roots and the ground, and I fell sound asleep right away. It seemed just moments later when he shook me awake.

"We have to get moving," he said. "You've been sleeping for half an hour. It's so cold you'll freeze. Come on now, get stirring."

I was cold, tired, and miserable, but staggered along hanging on to Papa's coat. How was it ever going to end? Papa said, "We could be near the Bedal home. I wonder if they could hear my pistol shots."

He fired off two rapid shots and waited. After a while he shot two more times, and then two more. We were lucky that he had plenty of shells with him. Some time later, we heard a shout. Papa shot twice again and gave an answering shout. Soon we saw a light and heard a crashing of brush. It was Harry Bedal, the oldest son, about 16. He had heard the shooting and knew someone must be in trouble. He had awakened his folks and went out to give whatever help he could. We were glad to be found and to come into a warm house. Mr. and Mrs. Bedal were up and dressed, but the four smaller children stood around in their nightshirts, gazing wide-eyed at the strangers coming into their home in the middle of the night.

Mrs. Bedal soon had my wet clothes off and wrapped me in a warm blanket. I fell asleep while eating a bowl of deer meat soup, as Mrs. Bedal was busy picking out devil's club thorns. She knew they work themselves into the flesh and have to come out right away.

When I woke it was early afternoon. Papa had been up a long time and was anxious to get back to our camp. After breakfast of mush and bacon, we started up the road to camp. "This has been a good lesson for me and for you, too, Elof," Papa said. "If I had not broken one of my own rules this would never have happened. Never, remember that, never go into the woods without candles so you can make yourself a bug to light your way."

We had gone quite a ways and Papa said, "Up there half a mile is the trail to the hermit's cabin. I dropped our fish poles when I lost the trail. I don't want to lose them, too."

I was still tired from last night's experience, but I did not want to lose our rods, either. They were the first boughten ones I'd ever had. They were the steel telescoping kind and I was proud of them. Mine had been given to me by a camper-tourist who had vacationed at Monte. Papa got his in Silverton.

We did not find the poles where we thought they had been dropped. Papa said, "We are closer to the cabin than I thought last night. If I had shot the pistol then, we might have awakened the man there. We'll go on up to see him and tell of our experience."

When we saw the cabin Papa stopped and hollered to let the man know someone was there. Papa said, "I don't want to startle a man living alone. He may not like strangers."

I expected to see some kind of strange character with a long beard, but he was just like anyone else, about thirty or thirty-five years old, a man who liked to live alone. He made his living helping Mr. Bedal part of the time, and spent the rest of the time hunting and fishing. It was a free life with few responsibilities. He had our fishing poles, which he had found that morning. We were glad to get them.

We stayed only a little while, just long enough to tell him of our experience last night and drink some coffee. The man would have liked for us to stay longer, but Papa was anxious to get to our camp. As we were about to go, Papa said, "Do you know what time it is? I forgot to wind my watch and it has run down."

The man stepped to the door and opened it so the sun could shine in, then said, "According to where the sun is shining on the cracks on the floor, it should be half past three. It's the only clock I have."

Papa looked at me and smiled. He set his watch, wound it, and we left. When we got home the next day, Papa's watch was off by only ten or eleven minutes. I guess the hermit's sundial was the only clock he needed. His time was his own, and he did not have to be anywhere at any particular time.

We found our camp in pretty sad shape. The storm had soaked our blankets. We hung them up and built a good fire to hurry up the drying out. We had no fish, however. The rains had raised the river and it was quite a flood. Our gunny sack with all our cleaned fish had floated away. After supper we wrapped ourselves in the dry blankets and went to sleep. It had not been a very successful or satisfying fishing trip.

After breaking camp the next morning, we tramped home without any more problems. Mama was surprised that we did not have any fish, so we had to tell the entire adventure. She looked at Papa and acted as if she wanted to scold him for letting us get into such a mess, but she was glad we had come out of it O.K.

We had another strange experience that summer. Papa and I were hunting about three miles from home. In a low marshy spot we saw some huge bear tracks. A bear usually weighs about 200 pounds. These tracks indicated that this animal could weigh twice as much. We hunted for more tracks, but did not see any more or any game, either.

The next day we borrowed a trap from Jim Kyes. It was a fearsome thing with iron teeth on the jaws. Using clamps, we set the trap and placed it on a moss covered log near the bear tracks in the marshy spot, and covered it with moss. Two saplings had grown up on each side of the log and we used these to hang bait. We hung a piece of bacon rind with wire so it was up six feet, directly above the trap. Our hopes were that a bear in reaching for the bait would put one of its hind feet in the hidden trap.

It was my job to go to the trap every other day. Nothing happened for several trips, then one day the bait was gone but the trap was not sprung. I was disgusted to have to travel home for more bait. Papa went back with me to see what had happened. The moss alongside the trap was disturbed, but the animal had not stepped in the trap.

Papa said, "We must have a pretty smart bear. Let's try hanging the bait a little higher so the bear will have to scramble around more in order to get it."

It was several weeks before the same thing happened again — the bait gone and no bear. When I told Papa he said, "Our plan is not going to work. We'll have to try something else."

We then placed the trap in the marshy spot with the bacon right on the trigger, without any covering. When the bear reached for the bait he would have to trip the trap.

Nothing happened for several weeks. I made the usual trips to the trap and it looked as if we would never catch that big bear. Papa said, "It is the wrong time of the year now. The hide won't be any good. Next time I go down that way I'll pick up the trap."

It was several days before we went fishing in Palmer Creek, two miles past the place where the trap was set. Papa was going to get the trap that morning, but the dew was so heavy that he decided to wait until after our fishing later that day.

We had very good luck with our fishing so we started home. As we approached the spot where the trap was, it was almost dark on the tracks and pitch dark in the woods where the trap was set.

I waited on the tracks while Papa went into the woods to the trap. It wasn't long before I heard a loud yell and a crashing of brush. I stood up as Papa came stumbling out of the woods. Without a word he motioned for me to come as he almost ran up the track toward home. I had quite a time trying to keep up with him.

I knew he was excited about something and wondered what had happened. We were almost home before he settled down enough to tell me what all the fuss was about.

He said he had parted the bushes to see into the clearing where the trap was, when suddenly a bear stood up with a loud roar, and with a front paw shook the trap almost in Papa's face.

"I was scared," he said. "And I'm not over it yet. The only thing I could think of was to get out of there."

I guess it was not funny for Papa, but I couldn't help giggling a little. He looked at me, and I wondered if he was going to be mad at me for laughing, but after a while he laughed a little, too. I guess he realized that it must have been funny to see him scrambling out of the brush in such a hurry.

Of course, we had to tell Mama and Ely about it. Mama said, "You sure get into the awfulest messes. You're going to have to learn to be more careful."

After a while, Papa and I went uptown to tell Mr. Kyes and Mr. Vogelsburg of our adventure. There were more smiles and chuckles as Papa told about how scared he was. As it was late, they decided to wait until morning to go after the bear. Next morning the bear was still there, but not so wild. A night's wait with a front paw in the trap had not been too pleasant. It was bawling like a calf that had lost its mother. Mr. Kyes asked me if I wanted to shoot it, but I shook my head. He then put the animal out of its misery with one shot of his .35 caliber Winchester. I did not want to trap any more animals.

We cleaned out the insides and tied the legs together so we could carry the bear home to skin it and divide it for all of us. We were glad to have the meat. Some was canned in quart jars and the rest salted down. It saved us many trips to Silverton for supplies.

21

High-strung Youngsters

It was getting closer to fall and some thoughts were being given to school for Ely and me. No teacher would be hired for two children. We could have gone to Silverton and boarded out with a family there, but my folks thought they would like it better if the Bedal children could come to Monte to go to school and board with us.

My father and Mr. Kyes were to go to the Bedal home to tell them of the changed plans for their two children. I coaxed my father to let me go along. I wanted to meet again the two children who were going to be with us for the coming school year.

The weather was cold when we started out. It had snowed a couple of inches the night before, but was clear now, with very little snow on the tote trail. Papa and Mr. Kyes wondered how Mr. and Mrs. Bedal would like to have their children coming to Monte instead of to Darrington, where they had been going to school.

As we came to the clearing where their home was, Papa shouted, "Mr. Bedal, Mr. Bedal, you have company." Faces showed at the window and Mr. Bedal appeared at the opening door.

"Why, Otto, you old mine-tender. What are you doing out in such weather?"

"It's good country weather," Papa said.

"It's cold, that's what it is," said Bedal. "Better come in before you freeze. I see you brought your skinny stringbean along. I see he looks all right after that adventure in the woods a couple of months ago."

"Yes, he's a chip off the old block," Papa said. "I don't think I have to introduce Jim Kyes. You must have known him a long time."

"Yes. Much longer than you."

Mrs. Bedal greeted us with smiles. She was glad to have company — it happened so infrequently. The four smaller children stood to one side, seemingly very shy. Harry, the oldest at seventeen, was a grown man. We had to have coffee and deer meat stew before any mention was made of the plan for the two school-age children.

A lot of discussion went on the rest of the day. The two children were told they were going to stay at our house while going to school at Monte for the following year. There was a great eyeing of each other and a wondering how we would get along. It would be a great change for all of us. I was glad for the companionship.

We stayed at the Bedals' that night, with Mrs. Bedal busy packing for the two children who were to come with us, one boy, eleven, and the girl, ten years old. The weather was much warmer, so traveling was better. When we got home that afternoon, Mama made the kids welcome. She gave them a room with two beds, so they could be together. Everything seemed to promise a very good time and companionship for us all.

Papa and I went to Silverton with the push car to meet the teacher who was expected. She was a small girl — I was taller than she. With her dark eyes and her black hair pulled straight back in a little knot, she looked almost Oriental. Her name was Miss Moncrief. Her home was in Everett, but she had never paid much attention to events or things at Monte Cristo, so on the way up the track Papa told her some of the history of Monte and of the things she could expect to see.

She walked part of the way, but with her thin-soled shoes she soon had to ride the push car most of the time while Papa and I pushed it up the grade. She marveled at the scenery and said how nice it must be to live in such a nice place. Wait until the snows come, I thought to myself, she might change her mind.

Mama was glad to see us come. I felt that Miss Moncrief and she would get along fine. She would be someone besides Mrs. Vogelsburg (who seldom came) to talk to. Jim Kyes and the Vogelsburgs also came to get acquainted. We had quite a good party.

School started as usual in the old schoolhouse. Either Mr. Kyes or Mr. Vogelsburg (who lived the closest) would start the fire each morning so the schoolroom was warm when we came in. Miss Moncrief had the same problems Miss Rice had, having to keep the four children busy the whole day. She, too, taught us drawing, basket weaving, clay modeling and knitting to keep us and herself busy.

Goto, the new Japanese caretaker at the Royal Hotel, came to school for a while. He said he wanted to learn to speak and write English better. I have always thought he was more interested in Miss Moncrief than in lessons, although she never gave him any encouragement. He made a clay teapot which he was going to give to the teacher, and was very disappointed when it broke while he was firing it in the abandoned kiln at the assay office. He didn't come to school very often after that.

Mama and Miss Moncrief became good friends. There was a lot of jabbering in the kitchen after school and in the evenings. It was enjoyable for all of us. What with visits with the Vogelsburgs and Jim Kyes, it was not lonesome despite the empty houses along Dumas and Mercedes Streets.

One thing marred the goodwill of us all that spring. I suspect it was my fault. The Bedal boy and I got into an argument over something or other and it finally developed into a fight.

We were both used to having our own way, and whatever the trouble was, it became quite a brawl. His sister entered into the squabble, too. Before it was over, we were all crying, but still mad at each other.

Mama and Papa didn't find out anything about this until later, but the next morning, when the two Bedal kids were not around anywhere, I had to tell Papa about the fight. Not only were they gone but their clothes were, too. Papa found their footprints in the little snow that was left here and there, leading down the tracks toward their home.

"They're heading for home all right," Papa said. "I had better go after them, so I'll know they get there O.K."

After getting some food together and some clothes that the kids had missed, he hurried after them. When he came back the next day, he said he had caught up with them just before they got to Barlow Pass. He had quite a time convincing them that he was not trying to get them to go back to Monte, but only going to accompany them to their home. They were determined they were not going to Monte and told Papa that he did not have to go with them the rest of the way.

When they all reached their home, the Bedals were not too surprised to see them. Mr. Bedal said, "I expected there might be a little trouble between two high-strung youngsters, but I thought they would work it out. Now that my kids are home, I will make other arrangements for their schooling, very likely in Darrington."

I felt bad over the fuss, which really started over nothing. The Bedal kids must have felt the same way because the next time I saw them they were friendly. Now only Ely and I were left to go to school. It was lonely at times.

Miss Moncrief left when school was over. When asked if she would be back, she said no, because she would be teaching elsewhere. She said the first year of her teaching career was quite an experience and she would never forget it or any of us. I did, however, manage to graduate out of the eighth grade, with every expectation of entering high school in Everett that fall.

22

The Man of The Family

When the receivership ended at Monte, my father lost his job. He walked the thirty miles along the tote road to Darrington to look for work. Mr. and Mrs. Vogelsburg walked over Poodle Pass to Index. Papa came back to Monte a few weeks later and told us that he had a job loading hand-hewed ties on railway cars. He didn't know how long the job would last, so he told us to stay at Monte until things were more settled.

He also said he had stopped at the Bedals' and Mr. Bedal had offered to sell him the back eighty acres of original standing timber for $300.00.

"I have been thinking about it," Papa said, "and it might be a pretty good proposition."

Mama said, "I know we have to move wherever your work is, but I dread to do so. We have had such a good time here with these nice people. If you decide to buy that timber, I suppose we would be near the Bedal home, wouldn't we?"

"That's right. As long as I haven't a job here we have to move somewhere. In the meantime you will have to stay here. It will be up to Elof to go to Silverton for supplies for the coming winter. He can do it. Don't worry, everything will turn out all right."

Papa went back to Darrington the next day. It was now my job to be the man of the family. I was busy cutting down trees and getting the wood into the basement for our winter's fires. I also made many trips to Silverton for supplies. I had found a short cut past the railway switchback so the trip to Silverton was only thirteen miles one way. I made the twenty-six mile round trip in one day. Sometimes I got tired when I carried too big a load. As always, my .22 rifle went with me as far as Barlow where I ditched it under Mr. Mackintosh's cabin, so I would be able to shoot any grouse I might see on the return trip.

Mama always had a letter for me to send to Papa whenever I went to Silverton, but only occasionally was there one from him. My work was pretty well caught up, so one day I asked Mama if I could walk over to Darrington to see Papa.

"You're getting pretty big for your britches, aren't you?" she said. "Just because you have been going to Silverton and back in one day, you think you can walk to Darrington. That's thirty miles."

"Yes, Mama, but I can stop at the Bedals' overnight. I know they won't mind. I will only stay a couple of days in Darrington."

I was allowed to go the next day. The trip wasn't bad at all; in fact, it was easier walking on the soft turf than on the gravel and ties of the railroad tracks.

Mr. Bedal was surprised to see me. He wondered what I was doing so far away from home.

"I am going to see my father in Darrington," I said. "Can I stay overnight?"

"Sure you can stay," he said. "There are just Harry and the two girls now. We had a bad accident. One of my boys drowned in a flood some time ago."

He looked away to hide his sorrow. I did not know what to say and hung my head. I knew that accidents could happen so suddenly in out-of-the-way places, and I vowed to be more careful in the woods. I learned later that the boy had gone out in the river to try to save some shingle bolts from the flooding waters. The boys had worked so hard to cut the shingle bolts and bring them to the river — it was a sad ending to their efforts.

I was made welcome at their home, with no mention of the squabble I had had with the two children at Monte or of the school there, only of what might be our future plans. Mr. Bedal reminded me that he had offered to sell some of his land to my father and said maybe we would be neighbors sometime in the future. I said as far as I knew, my father was still thinking about it.

I left the next morning. It was easy walking — the tote road from the Bedal's home to Darrington was more traveled than it was to Monte, and not so overgrown. I did not meet or catch up with anyone, but I was somewhat disturbed for a while by a cougar that followed me for several miles. However, I had Papa's .32-.40 rifle with me so there was no danger, and since there are plenty of deer around that part of the country, it could not have been hungry. I suppose it followed me out of curiosity.

It did not take me long to find Papa after reaching Darrington. He was still loading railway ties at the rail yard and was very much surprised to see me. His first thoughts were that something was wrong at home, but I assured him that everything was all right there. I had only come to see him and to see if things were O.K. with him. I was also curious to see the place where we all might live someday.

"I stopped at the Bedals' overnight," I said. "He wondered if you had made up your mind to buy some of his land."

"Yes, I have made up my mind," Papa said. "Bedal has raised the price to $350.00, and I think it is too much. What he wants to sell is farther away from the river. It will be a long time before that will be logged off, and in the meantime a forest fire could burn up all the timber."

That was one time that my father was mistaken. That tract of land and others were logged off not too many years later when a small railway was built to it. Then, one large cedar tree sold for more than the whole eighty acres cost in the first place.

Papa was going to start on a new job in a couple of days. He was going to help build a road into another stand of timber for hauling out the hewed ties. He had to blast some of the larger stumps out of the way. Some of the dynamite was partly frozen and did not always explode. To be on the safe side he built a fire and placed the powder near it to thaw. While he was away to dig holes under the stumps, it was my job to watch the fires.

Because of my inattention, the dynamite caught on fire. I ran, expecting an explosion. Nothing happened except the dynamite burned like stovewood. I hunted up Papa and told him what had happened.

He said, "You're lucky. Dynamite can be very unpredictable. The least jar or fire can set it off. Never fool around with powder."

I helped Papa dig holes under some stumps. Later when the woods workers had left their jobs, we used dynamite right out of the boxes. All the stumps blew up without any misfire.

That night Papa said, "When this job is over I will have a steady job at the sawmill. I will rent a house here and then come up to Monte to help with the moving. I know none of us likes to leave Monte Cristo, but this is where my work is so here we have to live."

I went back to Monte the next day, a little disheartened over having to move away from there in the spring, but at least knowing what some of the future held. I stopped again at the Bedals' and told Mr. Bedal what Papa had said in regard to buying the timber claim.

I think he already figured out what my father had decided, for he said, "Yes, I can see how he figures. It's too bad, though. It would have been nice to have close neighbors."

When I got home the next day I told Mama everything that had happened, and that Papa was going to have a steady job in the sawmill and we were going to move the next spring.

Mama looked a little downhearted and wondered how we could move our things, and what things we would have to leave. I knew how she felt. It is not easy to leave a home that one has been happy in.

★ ★ ★

I made the usual trips to Silverton for supplies, and always brought a letter for Papa. He did not write too often, but when a letter did not come for a really long time, Mama became worried that something was wrong. She wanted to go along on my next trip to Silverton.

I said, "I know you are worried about not getting a letter, but going to Silverton is not going to bring news any faster."

"Yes, I know, but I want to go anyway. I want to see other people."

"Mama, it is not easy to tramp those 26 miles on the ties."

"I still want to go. I can carry a few groceries, too."

We all went the next morning, walking slowly. Mama did not have hiking shoes, and I thought the gravel between the ties must be hurting her feet through her thin-soled shoes, but she did not complain.

When we reached Barlow Pass, the sun had come up and it promised to be a very warm day. I left my jacket and .22 rifle under Mr. Mackintosh's cabin, where I knew they would be safe, and we continued on.

As we went on, I noticed Mama and Ely were walking slower and slower. I guessed they were getting tired. I thought we might have to stay in Silverton overnight, although I didn't say anything. We had tramped about five miles from Barlow when Mama wanted to rest. We sat on the ties and ate some lunch that Mama had prepared.

After eating I said, "I am going on to Silverton alone. You must be tired. Take your shoes off and soak your feet in the little stream over there. When you are rested, you could start back home. I'll go fast and will catch up before long. Or you could go toward Silverton and stay the night there."

As I started down the tracks, I suddenly remembered I had left Papa's letter in my jacket back at Mackintosh's cabin at Barlow Pass.

"Oh, my!" Mama said. "What are you going to do?"

"There's only one thing to do," I said. "I'll have to go back to get it." Away I went, traveling fast, sometimes running for a ways.

Being alone in the mountain terrain, I thought of Mama's intuition of danger to my father. Was something like that possible? Wiping the sweat from my face with a shirt sleeve, I hurried on. Even at my faster pace the way seemed endless. I counted steps as I went. One hundred, two hundred, and so on until I lost count. I looked ahead to the next curve of the tracks, thinking that when I got there it would be only a little further. I still had to get back to our resting place and then on to Silverton. I thought again that maybe we would stay there overnight.

This is what it must have been like for the pioneers who first saw this expanse of wilderness. They probably thought they would never get back to civilization again, and some of them didn't.

I hurried on and on and finally saw the cabin. After getting the letter and having a cold drink of water from the creek nearby, I started back again, eager to get back to my mother and sister. I was a little surprised to see them still sitting where I had left them. They had gone neither of the ways I had suggested.

"What do you want to do, Mama?" I asked. "Do you want to go on to Silverton and stay for the night at the Hickeys', or do you want to start toward home? It's four miles to town and it's five miles to Mackintosh's cabin. I know we can stop there overnight."

"We'll start home after a while," Mama said. "If we go to Silverton, we would be that much farther away. Aren't you awfully tired after those extra miles?"

"I'm O.K., Mama. Start out when you feel like it. I'll hurry."

I reached town and got the necessary groceries and a letter from Papa, which I opened right away. Everything was all right with him. That made me feel better, although I still wondered about Mama's intuition of danger to Papa.

Hurrying faster toward home, it did not take me long to travel to where I had left Mama and my sister. They were still there. Mama's feet had swollen so she could not get her shoes on. They did not know what to do, and wondered if we would have to make some kind of camp and stay until Mama's feet were better.

I thought I had a better idea. I took off my undershirt and tore it into strips to wrap around Mama's feet. It was not enough, so I coaxed her to take off her underskirt and tear more strips. She could now walk, though the blisters hurt. She walked on the outer edge of the ties where there was less gravel. Ely and I cut some brush and swept off the larger pieces of gravel so Mama would not have to step on them.

It was very slow going, with rest periods quite often. The five miles to Barlow Pass were the longest miles I ever walked, and for Mama they must have been endless.

I found the hidden key to Mackintosh's cabin. We found everything as expected. Wood and kindling by the stove, quilts hung up in the ceiling to keep mice from building nests in them, and food stored in lard pails as was customary. I built a fire so we could heat water to bathe Mama's feet. While Ely did that, I prepared supper, mostly from our own supplies. After we had eaten we went to bed for a well earned rest. Ely and my mother slept in the two bunks and I rolled up in a quilt on the floor. Nothing could have kept us from sleeping that night.

Everyone felt better the next morning, and Mama's feet were much better. I had found some salve and she smeared some on before wrapping her feet up in the cleaned rags. The salve box had a horse on it, so I suppose it was for horses, but Mama said it was all right. At least she could get her shoes on.

After breakfast, I put wood and kindling by the stove and hung the quilts up and left everything as we had found it, and a note telling who had been there and why. I knew Mackintosh would understand and would not care as long as we left things straightened up.

We arrived home without any more difficulties, walking slowly because Mama's feet still hurt. She was glad to get there and vowed never again to make such a walk, at least not without decent shoes.

23

Darrington

A couple of weeks later we were surprised to see Papa coming up the walk. Sam Strom was with him. Papa had big news: he had a steady job at the mill in Darrington and he had rented a house. We were going to move! Not next spring as we had expected, but right now!

There was a great scurrying around and wondering about what we could take with us and what we would have to leave. The things we needed the most would have to be piled on the push car. That was only a wooden platform six feet by eight feet on four wheels. Someone, I guess it was Mr. Kyes, had "found" the "missing" or hidden wheel. (It had been missing because the boys or some hikers had used the car, and at one point, Mr. Kyes hid the wheel so the car could not be used that way.) Anyway, there it was sitting on the tracks, ready for us to load it.

Mama kept crying about leaving this or that, and Papa kept asking, "Where will we put it?" Mr. Kyes and Mr. Strom both helped us load up. Kyes was going with us to bring the car back. He would now be alone except for Goto, the caretaker at the hotel.

It took us two days to pack and stow things on the push car, which was piled six feet high. During this time Mama wanted to take more. She finally persuaded Papa that he would have to make a second trip to take the things put to one side. Then, at least, we would have enough furniture to get by in our new home.

During those two days came the most astounding news of all! Sam Strom told the story in fits and starts, while Papa tried to shush him. As I listened, I thought of Mama's intuition about Papa's being in danger. She had been right!

Papa had met Sam uptown and they had gone into a saloon to have a beer while talking. They were minding their own business when a burly stranger pushed Papa and said, "Move over, Bud. This is my seat!"

Papa looked at the bartender, who said, "Better do as he says. Wild Willy is a pretty rough customer."

"And if I don't?" Papa had said.

"And what if you don't?" repeated Willy. "Well, you had better have something to back that up," and took a wild swing at Papa who ducked and swung one of his own that sent Wild Willy on his back.

We all stared at Sam, who pretended to be busy packing.

"Tell us more. What happened? Tell us more."

"Well!" Sam said, "Willy got real mad. Furious at being made a fool of, but the drinks inside him made him stumble and Papa grabbed a good wrestling hold and threw Willy across the room where he lay with dark threats. 'I'll get you for this . . . you wait . . . I'll get you.' "

Sam stopped as if that was all, but he was just teasing us. Mama looked at Papa with astonishment. Jim Kyes chuckled and Ely and I coaxed, "Is that all? What happened after that? Tell us more."

"No, that's not all," Sam said. "I've known Wild Willy a long time, and he could be real mean. So when Otto said he was going to Monte to help you move, I decided to come along. I didn't trust Willy."

With us waiting with excitement, Sam filled his pipe, more to make us anxious than anything else, as he continued, "We had not traveled on the way to Monte very far, and when we rounded a sharp curve, there stood Wild Willy with a rifle pointed right at us. I took a step forward and said, 'Are you going to put that gun down, Willy?'

"Willy said, 'That ain't for you. It's for him. Stay out of this. I'm going to fix him.'

"By that time I had my pistol out," said Sam, "pointing it right at Willy.

"Willy took a step backward and stumbled. His rifle went flying down the bank and into the creek. He stood there a moment, then scrambled down to get his gun. We watched for a while, but he must have cooled off because he went through the woods toward Darrington."

We listened to Sam with astonishment and amazement and in wonderment that he had not told us this before. He said he had been wondering if he should tell it at all, but thinking it over, and against Papa's advice, felt that he could tell us because at some time we would find out anyway.

"We kept good watch the rest of the way here," Sam continued, "but no sign of Willy. I think we have heard the last of him."

We all wondered about that. Had we really heard the last of Willy? Was he the kind of man who would forget his anger? Would he have shot Papa if Sam had not been along? Only the future could tell us the answers to these questions. Leaving peaceful Monte Cristo and going to a place where we might encounter a man like Willy was not a very pleasant prospect.

We had everything that we could take loaded up the next morning. With Mama and Ely sitting on top of the huge load and Mr. Kyes braking on one wheel with a board, they started down the track. Papa and I were walking, and they were soon out of sight. Three miles away, near Weedin Creek, the tracks leveled and the car had stopped. They were waiting for Papa and me to help push until a down grade was reached.

Then the car would alternately speed out of sight on the down grades and stop on the more level places, waiting for us to help push again. We reached Silverton before noon. After unloading our things onto the station platform, we had lunch at the Hickey home, where Mama and Ely would stay. Then Mr. Kyes, Papa, and I pushed the car back up the track to Monte, where we arrived at dusk.

We loaded up the push car once again, and went to bed until the next morning. It did not take us long to get back to Silverton. After unloading the things, we watched Mr. Kyes trudge up the track pushing that precious car. He wanted to get back to his mine. All his life, his innermost thoughts had been of finding a rich gold mine. It would be a lonely place from now on, with only Goto for company. I knew his thoughts were not of loneliness, however, but of his mine.

Our whole family stayed at the Hickey home that night. (That home, by the way, is still standing, and will be kept up by a historical society.) We had a lot of talking about moving to Darrington and, of course, about Wild Willy, who was quite prominent in our minds.

When the train came the next morning, we loaded our things into a boxcar. Our stuff looked piteously small in that empty car. Mama kept wishing we had taken more of our things on the second trip. We arrived in Hartford early in the afternoon and found a room in a hotel to await the train to Darrington the next day.

Other people were also moving to Darrington and loaded their things in "our" boxcar. They talked with Mama and Papa about their plans and hopes in a strange place. They had only small children, so there was no one for me to get acquainted with.

At Darrington Papa got a horse and wagon to haul our stuff to our rented house. Mama showed her disappointment at the size of the place, and it was only when Papa said he was lucky to get anything at all that Mama seemed more satisfied. With a living room, a kitchen, and three bedrooms, it would do for us four. Beds were set up and the kitchen table and chairs were arranged. Luckily a large kitchen stove came with the house, so we soon were able to have something to eat.

Mama would have liked to scrub up the whole house, but there was no time for that. She grumbled a little about the smaller rooms, "but at least there won't be so much to clean. We'll get along. And we are a lot closer to a store than we were at Monte Cristo." She was already making plans for window curtains and other improvements she thought were necessary for good living.

The yard around the house was just dirt. No grass, shrubbery, or trees. A fence separated us from the gravel road to town. In back was a woodshed with the usual backhouse beyond.

Papa went to work the next morning, glad to be making some money. Mama cleaned house, while I went out to split the wood that had been brought from the sawmill. The wood would still have to be piled up in the shed.

Down the road past our house about a mile was an Indian village. The Indians went by our house quite often, sometimes on horseback and other times on foot. Mama was scared of them.

"They are not going to do us any harm," I said. "Their village is quite a ways down the road. We'll go down to visit sometime."

"Oh, no. I don't want to go. You can go, but I'm afraid of them."

"There are many tribes of Indians in America," I said. "They don't harm anyone. They sometimes get drunk on weekends, and do some yelling, but no war dances."

At times a group of them came past the house from town, especially at night, whooping and hollering, three and four on a horse.

Occasionally one fell off and we could see him sitting on the road, shouting for his companions to come back to pick him up. But they never did stop, just galloped merrily on their way, hooting and hollering. The poor unfortunate at times staggered down the road after the others, but more often lay down to sleep until morning.

It was several days before we went to town, a half mile away. Mama wanted groceries and material for curtains. That was a novelty for her which she had not enjoyed at Monte. She said, "It will be nice to pick out your own things, instead of sending for them from the Sears catalogue or Bruhn and Henry's."

We met other people in town and at the store. They said, "How-de," and went on their way, not a friendly "Hello" and a moment's chat like we had with the people at Monte.

"The people we met did not seem very friendly," I said, as we walked home. "I wonder why?"

"Perhaps they are not used to many strangers," Mama said. "Maybe they are clannish. Some people don't get friendly until they have known you for a long time."

In a few days our house looked more liveable. I had split all the wood and stacked it in the shed. There was still kindling to make, but I could do that any time. I was straightening my room one day when I spotted my fish pole.

"I want to go fishing, Mama," I said. "The river is just through the woods over there a little ways."

"All right," she said. "Don't get lost." She looked at me and smiled.

"Oh, Mama, you're teasing me. You know I won't get lost in the woods. I'll fish up to the swinging bridge and come home by way of the road."

I dug some worms in the back yard and had no trouble finding the river. I had not fished long when two boys my own age came along to fish, too. We fished close to each other for a while, then one of them said, "I'm George and this is my brother Frank. We live uptown. Where do you live?"

"I live on the road to the Indian village. My name is Elof. We just moved here. We came from Monte Cristo."

"Oh, yes. That's the mining town that went broke," Frank said. "There are mining claims over on Gold Hill, across the swinging bridge. Sam Strom has one. Do you know Sam Strom?"

"Yes, I know Mr. Strom very well. He is a good friend of my father. Sam gave me my .22 rifle."

"I've got a .22, also. We'll have to go hunting sometime," said Frank.

We fished some more. As we came in sight of the swinging bridge, the two boys left with enough fish, saying they had some wood to split and carry in the house. I continued on up to the bridge and was about to go home when a man came to fish, also.

He had a new pole and some artificial flies. I had never seen anything like that before and asked him about them. He said, "A man in Everett makes them. See? The red yarn is wrapped around the shank of the hook and is called the body, and the grey feathers are called the hackles. They are made to look like insects. There are different kinds of colors for different kinds of insects."

I watched him for a while, but he did not have much luck. He could cast the line almost across the river, but maybe he didn't have the right kind of flies. I started fishing with worms and caught a trout right away.

He said, "You're pretty good at that, I suppose you've fished around here a lot of times."

"No. This is the first time here. We just moved a few weeks ago from Monte Cristo. I did a lot of fishing up there. I think the fish like worms better than your flies."

"I guess you're right. I would like to try some worms. Maybe I can catch some fish, too."

I had enough fish, so when I left I gave him the worms I had. I was well satisfied, first with the fish I had caught and also with the two boys I had met. I felt everything was going to be all right from now on.

★ ★ ★

Papa brought Harry Bedal home with him one evening. He said, "Harry is going to work near town part of the time, while floating logs down the river from the logging camp. He wants to stay here when he can."

"Where will he sleep?" Mama asked.

"I'll get a bed for the living room. It's almost empty," Papa said. "I'll put a heater in there, too, when the weather gets cold."

So arrangements were made for Harry to eat and sleep at our house one or two nights a week. He brought his pinto pony with him. We had many good fishing trips along the river on that pony.

Harry was a wild rider. We rode through the brush bareback — Harry in front hanging on to the reins, with me hanging on to Harry, ducking low to keep from being swept off by low hanging branches.

He was a good fisherman. I learned a few tricks from him in getting bait grubs from rotten logs and finding all kinds of insects at different times of the year.

Harry had one superstition that made things bad for Mama. When he came home soaking wet from wading in the river or from rain, he crawled right into bed with all his clothes on. He thought if he changed into dry clothing, he would catch cold. It is true he never had colds, but it certainly was a mess for Mama to dry out the bedding. Nothing anyone could say would change his mind and Mama was glad that he wasn't at our house all the time.

★ ★ ★

Up the river from town was a dam part way across the stream. It was a salmon hatchery, with holding pens for the fish until they were ready for stripping. The females were killed when the eggs were ripe, and the males were milked (by squeezing their bellies) over the eggs. Then the eggs and "milk" were stirred slightly. The building held many small tanks where the fish were allowed to grow up to eight inches, then shipped to other waters that needed to be planted.

The dead salmon were given to a large group of Indians camped along the river nearby. They cut off the heads and then split the salmon up the back and smoke-cured them over alder wood fires. They got hundreds of fish so they would have plenty of food for the coming winter. Many times a large Dolly Varden was caught in the salmon traps. These trout were not kept but were thrown back into the river, or given to anyone who wanted them. I carried some home if I happened to be there when the men were dipping salmon out of the holding pens.

24

Goodbye Again to Such A Friendly Place

When school started I did not have to go because I had already gone through the eighth grade at Monte. But Papa thought I had better go anyway, so I could get better marks in grammar, which was my hardest subject. I had misplaced my report card, but told the teacher that I had gone through the eighth grade at Monte and wanted to go through again.

There were more than two dozen children in school that year (1907). All the grades were in one room, just as at Monte Cristo. Some of the students were Indians and they kept to themselves. I don't remember seeing any of the Bedal kids there. This surprised me somewhat. I suppose any of the ones who were of school age went to Silverton or perhaps did not go to school at all, which happened sometimes in those out-of-the-way places.

One group of children pretended to be rough and tough. They carried knives in holsters and threatened the Indians with them. I got a taste of them, too, because I was a newcomer.

"I don't play with knives," I would say. "I only use knives to skin animals and clean fish and whittle."

"Teacher's pet. Yeah, teacher's pet," they jeered, then turned to others.

The teacher tried to have the boys give up their knives while in school, but they just laughed at her and sometimes went home. The teacher was angry and reported the incidents to the school board. The kids came to school without knives after that, but that group of boys still gave the teacher some trouble. Seemingly for no reason, a fight would break out and she had no hope of stopping it. All the teacher could do was close the school and send us home. Things did get a little better as the year went along, but without the friendliness we had at Monte.

I didn't like many of the boys at school, but Frank and George were all the friends I wanted anyway. The school lessons, the chores, and fishing kept me busy and out of mischief.

I got along well with my school lessons. Some subjects I was behind in, especially grammar. Parsing and diagramming had always been hard for me, but the teacher was very patient and with her help I knew that I would pass my grades.

One bit of news which was a relief to us was that Wild Willy had been killed in a logging accident on the Skagit River. And there was other good news. Papa came home from work one evening almost bursting with it. He could hardly contain himself while telling us.

"How would you like to go back to Monte?" he asked. "It's not too certain yet, but there are stories that moneyed men are getting interested in the mines."

"If only we could," Mama said. "It was such a friendly place. It would be very nice if we could be in our old home."

"I don't want to raise any false hopes," Papa said. "I will write to Jim Kyes. He must be there at his mine, and he goes to Silverton at times. He will let us know what is going on. I want to go back and I can see that you all want to go, too."

School was almost over before we heard from Mr. Kyes. He said yes, the mines were going to start again, but advised us not to move until we heard from him again. Probably not until school was over. We were all excited at the news, and plans were made about packing. In a few weeks school would be over. Ely and I were both passing our grades. Papa was glad we all wanted to go.

It was a good thing we had only rented the house and would not be stuck with trying to sell it. We worried a little about our house in Monte and wondered if anyone were living in it. Papa reassured us that Mr. Kyes would take good care of it and would not let anyone move in.

Finally the day came to move. Everything had been packed except the beds and dining room table and chairs. We were just through breakfast when the horse and wagon came to take our things to the station. There was a lot of scurrying to get our stuff loaded and then unloaded into the boxcar.

The train soon came to hook onto our boxcar. We arrived in Hartford that afternoon, and had to stay there until the next day, waiting for the train to take us to Monte. Papa made sure our boxcar went along, too, and would not have to wait until another train came.

A lot more people were on the train to Monte. Lots of excitement! Gold was going to be mined again! The wildest kind of stories went from passenger to passenger. We smiled at each other, knowing full well that it was not so easy. We had experienced the hard work and frustrations of mining. Although the thoughts of these people were of gold, our innermost thoughts were of a job for Papa and of getting into our home.

Arriving at Monte was exciting. Jim Kyes and Mr. and Mrs. Vogelsburg were there to meet us and so were Jakey Cohen and Mrs. Sheedy. They opened up the Royal Hotel for some workers from the terminal and the concentrator.

We had lots of help to carry our things to our house. I peeked in the window. "It looks just the same," I said.

"Wait, I have a key," said Papa, as he opened the door and walked in. We hurried to follow, but stopped as the dead air and musty odors made the house seem strange to us.

"Come, let's open the windows," Mama said. "It will seem strange until we get the musty smell out."

To me everything was the same. This was home! We had expected that some of our furniture might have been taken, but everything was there.

I mentioned it to Papa and he said, "Well, Jim Kyes was here most of the time and then it is a kind of understanding that when some furniture is left, the owner has squatter's rights and will be back."

But I still wondered about this, because not all strangers would know about that.

A fire was started and coffee was made. Now was the time to hear all the news. Mr. Kyes and Mr. Vogelsburg alternated telling the latest developments.

The Guggenheims had picked up the smelter in Everett and some of the mines. A newly formed company, called The Monte Cristo Mining Company, with Mr. Colby, Mr. Hewitt, and others from Everett, bought the town site and some claims with close to a half million dollars invested.

Later the Monte Cristo Metals Company invested one and a half million dollars in other properties. The Northern Pacific Railway had improved the tracks and bridges and were able to keep a better schedule. The American Smelting and Refining Company bought some mines and the concentrating mill.

The geologists and mining experts convinced the owners there was untold wealth yet to be discovered at Monte. With all that money invested, everything looked rosy for the future.

Mr. Cook came back to run the donkey engine that hauled up the ore from the Rainey mine. His family did not come. Once again, Ely and I were the only children. That was all right by me — I was where I wanted to be. This was home!

Papa got his old job as tram tender at the terminal. The mines did not produce as expected and hoped for, but work continued. Some exploratory drilling in various places did not show any new veins of ore. The concentrator did not run steadily, but a full crew stayed. The train came only several times a week or when the loaded ore cars had to be hauled away.

The 45 Mine and the Bonanza Queen mine at Silverton were producing some ore, and the concentrator there was running. The train went there regularly.

With the smaller volume of ore being produced, the mine owners wanted the smelter to pay them for the arsenic in the ore, since it was worth something. This the smelter would not do. They said they were keeping the arsenic for themselves to help pay for the cost of extracting the other minerals, since there is an added cost to extracting minerals when arsenic is present.

The smelter in Tacoma *would* pay for the arsenic and so a few train loads of ore were sent there. But the extra cost of transporting the ore the greater distance cut the profits of the mine owners. More mines shut down. Papa lost his job as tram tender because the aerial tramways were not operating. The concentrator shut down, also.

Once again there were few people in Monte. Jakey Cohen and Mrs. Sheedy were gone and the hotel closed up. The Vogelsburgs had left some time ago, and the few miners at the Rainey kept house for themselves in some of the deserted houses on Dumas Street.

I graduated out of grade school in Monte and did not have to go to school any more, but I was expecting to go to high school next year in Everett. My sister was in a lower grade and was supposed to go to school. I do not know why she was not sent to Silverton that winter.

The Rainey mine was the only mine operating now, with Mr. Cook still running the donkey engine to hoist up the ore and dump it into the gondola cars to be sent to the smelter in Everett.

The donkey engine used wood for fuel, and Papa got a job falling trees nearby and cutting them up into cordwood lengths. He was paid $2.00 a cord. I helped him on the other end of the saw. It was cold and hard work that winter. We were lucky that it did not snow too much, although sometimes the fallen tree would bury itself out of sight in new snow and had to be shoveled out.

Falling the trees and cutting them into four-foot logs was not the hardest job — splitting the logs was the worst. We had no iron wedges and had to make them out of scrap iron found around the concentrator and hammer them out on the forge at the old blacksmith shop. After we split up the logs, we had to pile the wood in tiers to measure how much we had cut. We cut fifty-two cords. That was the only money made that winter.

Later in the spring, Papa got part-time work carrying the cordwood over the creek to the donkey engine and cutting it into the right lengths for the donkey. This gave him lots of time to go hunting and fishing and do some assessment on our claims. The summer went by fast. It was soon time to think about finding a place for me to stay while going to high school in Everett. I do not know what Papa was going to do to earn some money, but as long as Rainey was going, he was going to stay.

Little by little I began to realize that coming back to Monte Cristo was to bring only a second farewell. Coming back had given me a chance to relive a portion of my life that was dear to me, and I treasured it. I was growing up, somewhere between man and boy. Going to high school next fall would change my life a great deal. For the better, I hoped.

25

Everett

I knew leaving Monte would be a heartbreak, but it was my choice. The other time we had had to go because of Papa's job, but this move was so I could continue my education, and would be part of growing up. Papa and I then left for Everett.

Arriving in Everett in the early afternoon, we first got a room at a small hotel where we could stay while looking for a place for me to live. Looking through the ads in the paper, *The Herald*, Papa found one that seemed to be just for me. It said, "Have room and board for young man going to school."

Not knowing the names of the streets, we asked some people where 2521 Rucker was, and were given directions. Coming to the house, we saw it was a two-and-a-half story home.

When we rang the bell, the door was opened by a pleasant woman in her early fifties. She said her name was Mrs. King.

Papa said, "Do you have a room for my boy who is going to school this fall?"

"Yes, I do, if he doesn't mind sleeping in the same room with my grandson. He is going to school this fall, also."

I looked in wonder as we entered the hallway. The furniture in the adjoining room shone with high polish. The dark wood of the newel post and the balustrades led to the rooms upstairs. The room I was to share on the top floor was large enough for two beds and two dressers. Part of the ceiling slanted, but was high enough to stand up in. Papa said, "It is very nice. I wonder if I can afford it."

"I charge $17.50 a month for room and board and washing, if your boy will help my grandson split and pile wood for the stoves."

"Oh, he can do that all right. He has done plenty of that at Monte."

Papa paid Mrs. King for the first month's rent. Then we shook hands like two grown men and he left for the hotel room, until the next morning when he could get the train for Silverton and then make the fourteen-mile hike to Monte. I went upstairs to unpack the few things I had brought.

I met the other boarders that evening at supper. There was Mrs. Foster, a widowed daughter of Mrs. King; Mr. Frankemount, who was going to teach manual training at the new Washington grade school; and a lady whom everyone called Miss Princess, because she did not wear the usual skirts and high-neck blouses, but wore form-fitting dresses with low necks. Then Mr. and Mrs. Greenburg, newly married. He owned a men's clothing store on the northeast corner of Oakes and Hewitt, called the Red Front.

Of course, the one I was most interested in was Colin Headlee, Mrs. King's grandson, the boy I was going to have as a roommate for the coming school year. He was the same age as myself (15), but he was smaller than I was. I guess we eyed each other up pretty well while eating supper.

I was most embarrassed at supper. The meal was served in courses. Not having had a meal served in courses before, I was confused at the array of knives, forks, and spoons on each side of the plates. I watched the others to see what utensil to use next, so got by all right. The next day Mrs. King came out in the woodshed where I was chopping wood, and arranged pieces of kindling on the chopping block to show me what I should use and when. I got along better after that.

After supper, or rather I should say dinner, Colin and I went upstairs to get more acquainted. His father and mother were separated. His father lived on a ranch east of the mountains where Colin had dug up some Indian arrowheads. He had also found a bleached-out human skull in the same place. His mother was a Chautauqua lecturer and traveled all over.

Of course, I had to tell him all about Monte Cristo and what had happened to the mines. Also about hunting and fishing, which he did not seem to care too much about. We had a good time getting acquainted. I was lucky having found such a nice place to stay.

I went to register for high school the next day. When asked where I had gone to school and about a report card, I said I had no report card and had gone to school at Monte Cristo and through the eighth grade at Darrington.

They told me that I could not register for high school without a report card, and that the schools in Monte Cristo and Darrington were not accredited. However, in a couple of days I could take an examination at the County Courthouse, and if I passed I could come back to register.

I went back to the boarding house. I was very disappointed. I had not thought much about my former lessons during the past year. If I had known about a test I could have studied some and been more prepared. I was most worried about grammar. Math, geography, history, or spelling did not bother me too much, but grammar, I thought, wow!

"What is the matter?" asked Mrs. King, noticing my downcast expression. "Are you homesick?"

"No. I like it here," I said. "I have to take a test at the Courthouse, and I am afraid I won't pass. I haven't looked at a book for a whole year."

"Oh, is that all?" said Mrs. King. "You look like a bright boy. You should have no problem. Study all you can until you have to take the test."

I went to my room and thought about how kind Mrs. King was. I was lucky to be here. I got paper and pencil and wrote down all the things I could remember, especially about grammar. I did not sleep much that night, but that didn't help any.

In a couple of days a notice came for me to appear at the Courthouse for my test. As I walked the streets to what I called the Moment of Truth, I thought of the buildings and the people who had built them. They had passed their grades and so would I!

I felt rather small, however, when I entered the building, and even smaller when the instructor gave the test papers. There were others from the same kind of school that I had come from. They would have the same problems as I had, so I wasn't alone in that. I wondered how many would pass. In a way it was like going to the dentist that time in Seattle.

It took several days to complete all the tests. I was impatient, and would rather have had the suspense over with. That was not to be, however. The papers were all turned in, then there were several days of waiting for the mailman. I watched him come down the street and shivered when he handed me a letter. This was the news, good or bad. I still hesitated to open it.

Mrs. King said, "Open it, open it, see what it says."

Quickly I read down the page to grammar. It read F. "We are sorry to inform you that you have failed to pass the entrance examination."

"It says I have failed. I can't stay here. I have to go home and tell them I have failed."

"That's too bad," said Mrs. King. "I'm sure your father will understand."

"But after all the trouble of making the arrangements. I hate to tell them that I have failed," I said. "It will be such a disappointment. I guess I had better start packing my things for the trip home."

"I feel sorry for you," said Mrs. King. "I will not charge you for the days you have been here. You will need that money for other expenses."

26

"What in The World
Are You Doing Back Here?"

I caught the train for Silverton the next day, arriving early in the afternoon. I started trudging up the track toward home, carrying my belongings. It was a dreary trip. The closer I got to home the worse I felt. What were they going to say to me? That trip was the loneliest fourteen miles I had ever walked.

All was seemingly quiet when I went up those last few steps. Perhaps no one was home. I opened the door, and the faces of my father, my mother, and my sister turned toward me in astonishment.

"I had to pass a test and I didn't pass in grammar," I blurted out. "I'm sorry I didn't make it."

My father was speechless for a moment, then the meaning of what I had said sank in. "You didn't pass in grammar? You mean you can't go to high school this year?"

"Yes, that's right," I said. "I am sorry for all the trouble I caused. I studied till I was dizzy. I wouldn't know a part of speech from a cougar track."

"Well, something ought to be figured out. You and Ely have to go to grade school somewhere. Maybe it would be a good idea for you to go back to Everett. If you pass there you could go right into high school without a test. You know they won't hire a teacher for one pupil.

"Maybe you can still get your room at Mrs. King's and Ely can go there, too," Papa continued. "It would be nice if you could both be together instead of having Ely in Silverton and you in Everett."

Mama and Ely listened in surprise. Mama said, "Yes, that would be nice." My sister's expression showed that she would be glad, too.

"You start for Silverton early tomorrow, Elof," Papa said. "I don't know how the trains run from there, so you will have to figure things out."

"I know, Papa," I said. "There is no train tomorrow, but a work train is laying rip-rap along the river near Silverton. I talked with some of the crew and they said they would be through and be heading back to Everett tomorrow. I can get a ride with them when they go, and it won't cost me anything."

"Well, that's figured out," Papa said. "When you get to Mrs. King's find out if you can stay there and if Ely can stay, too. Write right away. I will be going to Silverton in four or five days. You should have a letter written by that time."

I was up early the next morning, full of hope that everything would turn out as we had planned. The walk to Silverton seemed like nothing this time. The rip-rap crew was working a short distance out of town, and I talked to the foreman about a ride to Everett. That was no problem. He wanted to know all about how I happened to be there and I told him about the circumstances and problems related to going to school. I also watched the workers getting huge boulders brom the mountain to lay along the river bank, to prevent the floods from washing the rails away.

I arrived in Everett at dusk with no charge and with the good wishes of the train crew. Hurrying to the boarding house, I arrived just in time for supper. Mrs. King was surprised to see me. "What in the world are you doing back here? I thought you would be at Monte Cristo."

"I was home, but Papa sent me back. He wants me to go to grade school here. Can I have my room back? Can my sister stay here, too, while she goes to school?"

I then explained why my sister wanted to come to school here, too. Mrs. King understood it all. She said, "Yes, you can have the room with Colin, and your sister can have the other attic room across the hall from yours. It will be nice for you to be together."

I was glad that things had turned out as Papa had planned. I wrote a letter and went to the post office right away, so Papa could get it as soon as possible.

I was able to enter the Lincoln grade school (which was located where the present high school auditorium is now), although I was several days behind the other pupils. The teacher started me in a lower grade, but soon realized I was able to do the eighth grade lessons. I quickly caught up with the rest of the class. I had been over much of the same lessons twice before, once in Darrington and then again at the Courthouse, so I did not have to study too hard.

About ten days after I started school, Mama and Ely arrived. I had been expecting my sister, but was surprised to see my mother. She said, "I didn't want Ely to come by herself. She's too small to come all that way alone. Can I stay here until I can get a train back home?"

"Of course you can stay here," said Mrs. King. "There are two beds in the room your daughter is going to have. You are welcome."

The next morning I took Ely to school with me. She was able to sign up for some class or other and started right away. I met her after school and she said that everything turned out all right.

I half expected that Mama had gone back to Monte Cristo, but when we came from school she was still there. What surprised me most was that she and Mrs. King were talking about cooking dinner. They had decided that Mama was going to stay for the school year and do the cooking for all of us. It was going to be different than cooking for a bunch of miners, but with the help of Mrs. King, I knew that everything would go along all right.

My father was not making much money working part time at the Rainey, but with Mama earning money cooking for Mrs. King, all our expenses would be paid.

The cost of board and room for Ely and me was $35.00 a month. The school board paid half of that because we were still in grade school, and it was cheaper than hiring a teacher for just the two of us wherever we stayed.

To help out with other expenses, Mrs. Foster got me a job at Mrs. Painter's Ladies' Hat Shop. My job, after school and on Saturdays, was to deliver hats to the customers, and to wash the store windows once a week. My pay was $10.00 a month.

Mrs. Painter sold mostly very expensive, made-to-order hats. Several women worked in the back room making them, covering the wire frames with silks and velvets and decorating them with flowers, feathers, and ostrich plumes.

The working men's wives could not afford to buy these hats. With wages from $1.75 to $2.00 a day, there was not too much money for fancy hats.

When I delivered a hat, I had to collect for it, sometimes with much argument from the husband. But I always got the money.

Most of the hats sold by Mrs. Painter went to women who lived in what were known at that time as "cat houses." The fanciest "houses" were on California street, where *The Herald* offices are now. There were always men sitting in the parlors, drinking and talking business. It seemed that those places were their recreation spots. Sometimes it was embarrassing for both of us when I saw a man from a business house uptown. Then they would swear at the women and yell at me to "get the h--l out of there."

The other cat houses were over on State Street and Hewitt. A square block was fenced in by eight-foot-high walls, and a man was at the gate. Inside were a number of one-room huts occupied by women. They always treated me all right, and sometimes gave me a quarter for delivering the hats.

Walking all over town delivering ladies' hats, I became acquainted with a great number of people and business houses. There were more saloons than any other kind of business — Everett had over forty saloons. On Bayside, in the western part of town, all of them were on the north side of Hewitt. This was known as the men's side. The department stores were on the south, or women's, side of Hewitt. I didn't blame the "nice" women for not going on the north side, with their long skirts dragging in the gobs of tobacco spittings or their bumping into an occasional staggering drunk.

Riverside was the older part of town. There all types of businesses were on both sides of the streets. Most of the sidewalks were cement, but the streets were planked so the horses could get a good footing while hauling the heavy loads.

By a vote of the people, Everett went dry the following year (1909). The city went broke because it lost a yearly $1,000 tax on each saloon. Donations were asked from business houses and individuals. The school children were also asked for nickels and dimes.

Since the city had no money for street sweepers, the gutters became full of horse droppings; and when the wind blew, it was a mess. This lasted for two years, until the saloons were voted in again. Marysville had stayed wet, and during Everett's dry years, traffic was heavy on the railroad tracks on weekends. Snohomish also had saloons. The interurban trains were plenty busy carrying passengers, with much hilarity on the return trips. There was a lot of complaining about the loss of business in town.

27

Another Goodbye, Another Home

My father had not come to Everett that year, and letters were few. Traveling the fourteen miles to Silverton was too much of a trip to make very often. My mother was lonesome for Papa, especially on the holidays. She was not feeling too well, either. She had not been too well at Monte, and she had worked hard with the housework and cooking for our boarders. Very seldom had I seen her sitting down except to sew or darn socks, or knit.

Looking back, I suppose we were not always very helpful — our thoughts were more on playing. She was only forty-four, but hard work and the lack of proper doctor's care when needed were taking their toll. I vowed to be more helpful whenever I could.

When school was over we made preparations to go home. As the train came closer to Silverton, I thought Mama's smiles were a little brighter. Papa met us there. He noticed Mama did not look so well, and said, "Maybe the city life did not agree with you."

But he had news for us. "Everything has closed down at Monte. I have a steady job in Gold Basin, at a sawmill." Who was to know whether this was for better or worse? Only time could tell. Papa's job was there, and there we would live.

"Mr. Kyes came with me," Papa said. "We brought one load of furniture. You can all ride the push car up to Monte. One more load of goods is all we can take."

We stayed at the Hickeys' overnight again. Their home seemed to have become a boarding house for the Normans in their trips to and from Monte. We were always welcome, and sometimes wondered how we would ever pay them back.

The trip up the track was uneventful. With Mama and Ely riding and the three of us men pushing, we made good time.

It was a sad visit. We had come home, only to go away again. Monte Cristo had been our home, our refuge in this new land, with many pleasant memories. Now we were leaving to go to a new place and strange people.

We wondered what our house in Gold Basin would be like, and if the people there would be friendly. For myself, it would not be for long. In the fall I would be going to high school in Everett and to the boarding house where I had been before. My parents and Ely were the ones who had to face the more uncertain future.

The loading of our things was completed the next morning, and there was nothing to do but to start coasting down the tracks. We were all a little downhearted as we looked back at a home we would very likely never see again. Mr. Kyes came along to bring back the push car.

The trip to Silverton was uneventful. All of us rode and we made good time, coasting most of the way. Our things were unloaded to await the train to Gold Basin. There were tears in our eyes as we watched Mr. Kyes push the car up the lonely track, out of sight.

Arriving in Gold Basin, we moved into a two-room log cabin with a lean-to, on a small meadow owned by Mrs. Hemple. The two rooms were large, but nothing like what we had at Monte. Papa looked at Mama and realized how disappointed she must be.

"It's the best I could do," he said. "At least I have a steady job. Some day we will have something better."

"Oh, I'm not complaining," Mama replied, and again said she was glad to be near a grocery store. "Those trips to Silverton always worried me."

We all chipped in to clean out the house, then started carrying our things, piece by piece, into our new home. But I could see Mama was not feeling very well, and I wished I could do something to help her. Only a doctor could do that.

The sawmill where Papa was going to work was across the tracks from Mrs. Hemple's grocery store. The cook shack and the bunk house were near the mill. The logs were cut high up on the mountain, and came down to the millpond by way of a very steep chute made of logs. Occasionally the haul-back cable could not hold the logs, and they would break loose and go speeding down the steep incline — at times the friction would cause the chute and the logs to catch on fire, or at other times the logs would jump out of the chute into the woods. When these things happened, the donkey engine went "Toot! toot! toot!" to warn everyone either to run away or to look for fires in the chute.

To help out with expenses for the coming school year, I got a job as bull-cook at the cook shack. My job was to help the flunkies peel vegetables, chop wood for the cooking fires, and sweep out the loggers' bunk house.

My most important other job was to carry out the noon meal to the loggers, a half mile up the mountain. The cook prepared the food I was to take, put it in pails and buckets, and hung them on a neck yoke for me to carry to the log chute.

At the bottom of the chute was a half log about eight feet long, hollowed out like a canoe. This was called a pig. After loading the food and myself into the pig, I pulled the wire fastened to the whistle on the donkey, and the haul-back cable pulled me up to where the meal was to be served.

I started a fire and filled a fifty-pound lard pail with water, poured in a pound package of coffee, and watched until it came to a boil.

Under a shed nearby was a long table and benches. I found tin plates and cups in a cupboard, with knives, forks, and spoons. I set the table and waited for the donkey engine whistle to blow. If I didn't have everything ready then, I'd have to run for the woods.

The loggers were big eaters and I had as many instructions on how to make good coffee as there were workers. They tried the usual tricks on me that they tried on all newcomers. One said, "Say, Sonny, bring up a dime's worth of hen's teeth next time, will you?"

Then another said, "Yeah, I forgot my left-handed monkey wrench this morning. Bring it up when you come."

Still another, with chuckles, would shout, "That half round square should be here now, look for it."

This was only in fun and just part of growing up. I would very likely play these same tricks on someone else sometime.

When the whistle called the men back to work, I cleaned up the dishes, and put the garbage out on a pile behind the shed. A little black bear came at times to scratch around for the leavings. It seemed to be harmless but I kept my eyes on him. I had been told by the camp cook not to bother or kill the bear. He was a good scavenger.

This job lasted the entire school vacation. I got $45.00 a month. Since I paid only $17.50 a month for room and board in Everett, and with the job at Mrs. Painter's hat shop, I was pretty well fixed for a while.

Even with all the work I had to do, I still had lots of time in the evenings to go fishing in the river, almost next door, which I always enjoyed.

I do not remember too much about the people at Gold Basin. Mrs. Hemple rented out a couple of sleeping rooms above her store. Her husband had been killed some years past, and she lived in her home behind the store with her two school-age children, Tony and Lenora, and her nephew, Waldo Rhodes. As I was busy working, I did not concern myself with any of the other people. But I do remember the wonderful raisin pies the camp cook made. I had my share of them.

★ ★ ★

When we left Monte Cristo, we all thought we would never see it again. But we were to make one more trip up there, our first home in this new land. During the many talks with Mrs. Hemple, my mother mentioned Monte so often that Mrs. Hemple said she would like to go up there and see for herself what it was like.

"I know you would like it," said Mama. "But I don't see how we can."

"I know how we can go," said Mrs. Hemple. "I have a horse and we can borrow a push car and all ride up, with the horse pulling."

"That would be wonderful," said Mama. "I hope we can."

Plans were made to go the next Sunday. Papa and I would get off work for a few days, so we could go, too. The horse walked slowly and we enjoyed the ride. Some of us walked at times so we could pick some berries, then hurried to catch up with the others.

We reached Silverton that evening. We were in no hurry — this was a pleasure trip, and we did not want to tire the horse or ourselves.

We stayed at the Hickey home again. I have a warm feeling for those wonderful, friendly people who sheltered us on our numerous trips to and from Monte Cristo, and listened to our many problems.

Starting out the next morning, we took our time again. Our first stop was the place where Mama and Ely had rested on that eventful trip when I had left Papa's letter in my jacket pocket, five miles back, and had to walk an extra ten miles to get the letter mailed. The story of this event has been told many times, with chuckling pleasant memories. (Several years later the Rucker Brothers built a lodge in that spot. They constructed a gas powered car, called the Galloping Goose, to carry their guests to the lodge and cabins there.)

After our next stop, at Barlow Pass, we reached Monte in the afternoon. To me it was a wonderful feeling, yet sad, knowing that this was only a brief visit. I was older now and would soon be going back to Everett and a new life.

As we walked the raised walkway to our house, I wondered what Mama's feelings were. On opening the door we just stood and looked. It was disappointing. Where there had been gladness and sadness there was now only an empty shell filled with cobwebs and dust.

We wandered through the rooms, with many thoughts. Mrs. Hemple wanted to know so many things and kept talking to make us forget some of our sadder memories. Mama wanted to leave right away, but it was too late in the day.

Jim Kyes was in town. He had just come in from his mining claim for supplies from his store. He was glad for our company, and wanted to hear all the news. He still had great hopes for finding some rich ore. This was an old story among those who hunt for that elusive metal called gold, an old story to be repeated many times to themselves and to others. Very seldom were these hopes fulfilled at Monte Cristo.

We had supper with Mr. Kyes that evening, then went back to our house to sleep, wrapped in our blankets. After breakfast with him the next morning, we made preparations to start back.

The return trip was on the down grade, so we tied the horse behind the car. We all looked back to get a last glimpse of our home and the lonesome figure of Mr. Kyes, waving until we were out of sight around the curve of the track.

Even with our braking one wheel, the horse had to trot at times to keep up with us. We stopped quite often to let him rest, while we picked some berries. We stopped only a short time at Silverton, just long enough to say hello and goodby to the Hickey family, and then we made good time, arriving in Gold Basin that evening.

It had been a memorable trip. For my mother, it was the last time she was to see that first home we had in America. She missed those kind neighbors she would never see again. It had been a good life there despite the hard work.

Although Mama was not well, she seemed to be feeling better — perhaps that medicine from Granite Falls was doing her some good. I did, however, notice she walked slower, and helped her whenever I could.

With the coming of fall, my thoughts were of Everett and high school. I felt I had wasted a year by having to go through the eighth grade twice, so I was determined to take enough studies to be able to pass through high school in three years instead of the usual four.

28

New Clothes

Arrangements had already been made for me to stay at Mrs. King's boarding house, and I was glad to be back. Mrs. King was glad to see me and asked about my family, but especially about my mother's welfare. I told her my mother was not too well, but had hopes the medicine from the doctor would help her.

Colin was in our room when I went up to put my things away. We had lots of things to talk about, he of his experiences at his father's ranch east of the mountains, and I of my job as bull-cook at Gold Basin.

At the dinner table I became reacquainted with Mrs. Foster, Mr. Frankemount, who had come back to teach again at Washington School, and Mr. and Mrs. Greenburg. There was one face missing, that of Miss Princess.

After we had eaten, Mr. Greenburg called me into his room. I wondered what he wanted to talk to me about.

He said, "I don't want to embarrass you by being too personal, but I couldn't help notice you are still wearing bib overalls. Is that what you are going to wear in high school?"

"Yes," I said. "I have no other pants. This is what I have to wear."

"You should have something more suitable in high school or else you will be made fun of. I would like to fit you out with something at my store. I will give you a good price. Come down tomorrow. I'll fix you up."

I would certainly like some new clothes. Buying them depended on whether I got my old job at Mrs. Painter's hat shop or some other job. That would be the first thing to do in the morning. Mrs. Painter assured me I could have the same job I had last year, and I could start the following Monday.

Next I went to Mr. Greenburg's store. He was not busy so he took me over to one corner and said, "I have some smaller sizes here. Let's see if we can find something to fit you." He had several my size and I picked out a dark gray suit. The trousers had to be shortened, but Mr. Green-burg said he would get that fixed up right away. Before he was through, I was fitted out with a new pair of shoes, two starched-front shirts, and a porkpie hat. I began to worry about cost, but when he said the whole outfit only cost $8.35 I was really tickled.

I felt grown up. I had bought new clothes all by myself! I went to the boarding house thinking I was pretty big. When I entered the house, Mrs. King said, "My, look who's here. You certainly are dressed up. Colin, come down, see Elof in his new outfit."

Colin came down, but new clothes were nothing special as far as he was concerned. I strutted a little just the same. I had another surprise that evening. When Mr. Greenburg came home to dinner, he brought an extra pair of trousers. He said, "I want you to have these to wear for everyday with your jacket. Don't thank me, just wear them."

I had already registered to go to school. The new high school on Colby had not been completed, so I had to go to the old wooden buildings at 25th and Oakes until the new school would be ready, possibly after the Christmas and New Year's holidays.

I got along fine with my extra studies, although I had only one study period a week in school. All the rest of the time was spent in class work. My job at Mrs. Painter's Hat Shop kept me busy until supper time, so all the other studying had to be done in the evenings in the back parlor. The only light was a small electric globe hanging from the ceiling. My eye began to bother me before I was through studying at ten or eleven o'clock. However, after a good night's sleep I was again ready for a day's class work, then off to the hat shop and more deliveries.

I met one other Norman in school. But his origin was Norwegian and his father owned the Norman suit house, so we did not have too much in common. One pleasant friend was Alma Hickey from Silverton, at whose house we had stayed so many times. She was a little younger than I, but had caught up with me because of my failure to pass out of the grade school the year before.

We met occasionally between classes. She approached me one day to ask me if I had the answers to our geometry lesson. I had no trouble with math, so I said, "Sure, I'll slip you a copy of them before the class." I was very pleased that I could in some way give help to someone who had helped us in the past. This passing of notes worked fine for several months, until one day the teacher asked her to go to the blackboard to explain to the class how she had arrived at the answer to the problem.

Alma tried hard, but the further she went, the more confused she became, and she started crying. I stood up, red-faced, to admit that I had given Miss Hickey the answers. We were kept after class and given a good lecture. I told the teacher why I wanted to help Alma; he said he understood my motive, but made us promise not to do it again. He gave us both a zero, besides.

Alma did not stay in school many weeks after that. One week she was there and the next week she was gone. I guess she went home to Silverton. I never saw her again. I had learned a good lesson: never cheat, no matter how much you want to help someone.

After the New Year's holiday we moved into the new school on Colby. I had a shorter walk to classes, but the routine was the same. Work after school and the long studies after dinner. My grades were all right. I was going to pass out of my freshman year O.K. I was going to have plenty of credits and I was looking forward to going home to Gold Basin after school was over for the year.

29

A Lonely House, A New Life

Everything was about the same when I got home to Gold Basin. But Mama looked older and moved a little slower, and it was a worry for all of us. I wondered why something couldn't be done to make her feel better. I suppose Papa was doing all he could, and it was up to the doctor from Granite Falls to give her all the help he could.

I got back my old job as bull-cook at the logging camp. Who had that job while I was in Everett I do not know, but I had no trouble in going to work as if I had never been away.

One evening as I was coming home from work, my sister came down the road to meet me. There was no happy shout or wave. As I came closer, I saw she had been crying.

"What is it? What is the matter?" I asked.

"Mama is in great pain. She is very sick. The doctor is with her, but he doesn't seem to be able to help her," Ely sobbed. "The pills ease her pain, but she must hurt awful."

"Mama was always so strong," I said. "I can't imagine she is really sick."

It was with a heavy heart that I entered the house. There was no sound, either, as I approached the bedroom. The doctor was there closing his bag. He said, "Your mother is in a coma. I have done all anyone can do for her. She will feel no pain."

"Mama, Mama!" I cried. I wanted to hold her, but went instead to Papa who was kneeling by the bed. I knelt by his side, looking at Mama so still, hoping for some sign of recognition. There was none as I touched her hand.

"I don't think she knows I'm here," I said at last. I did not really want to leave the room, but I did not want to stay either, for reasons I could not explain. I was drawn to the front room, and sat down in Mama's favorite chair. It was then I sensed her presence, not lying ill in the bed, but alive and speaking to me clearly! "We have had many good times together, my son. I would not want you to grieve for me now. There is so much in your life, so much in your future . . .''

I turned as a motion from the other room caught my attention. No, it couldn't be that. I looked tearfully at the doctor, then to Papa, and to Ely. The doctor nodded. "Yes, your mother is dead." Papa looked down without a word, and Ely sobbed silently.

Our mother was buried a few days later in Everett. It was within a week of the time that school was to start, so I did not go back to Gold Basin, but went directly to Mrs. King's boarding house.

My father and Ely went back to a lonely house. I was very sorry for my sister. It was her job now to keep house without a mother, as well as go to school. It would be almost too much for a thirteen-year-old girl. I wished and hoped she would get help from Mrs. Hemple and comfort from our father.

I thought a lot about my mother during those days in school. I thought more and more about the hard life of anyone following her man to faraway places. It was the woman who held the family together, thinking only of them as she labored, helping him make a home. It was to her, as wife and mother, we all turned in times of stress. Many words have been written, but not enough, of the courage, the stamina, and the helpfulness of these pioneer women. It is hard to realize the hardships they endured.

I continued in school, although things were not going too well. The extra studies seemed harder. Studying in the back parlor in the evening with the poor lighting made my eye worse. I now wore glasses, but they did not help much. The blackboard was harder to see. Perhaps, I thought to myself, I had lost the determination, the courage, to complete my goal. I did not want to become a laborer without schooling, as my father had been. I realized the only way to a better life in the future was schooling, so I continued.

I received a yellow slip the last semester; and if I got another I would not pass. My eye was increasingly painful. I was becoming more discouraged. By the end of the term, I knew I would not pass.

During the last months of the school year, the saw mill at Gold Basin closed down. My father and Ely moved to Granite Falls and my father worked at the Waite sawmill. He lived on a small "stump" ranch near the mill, and my sister was boarding with a family closer to the school. Now that my father was alone and I had not passed, I decided to stay with him and get a job at anything I could find. He was glad I came to stay with him, but sorry I had quit school. I told him I would try laboring to improve myself, working with my hands instead of with my head.

I went to work right away, piling blocks for the shingle sawyers. The work was very hard, almost too much for my young muscles. The twenty cents an hour was a disappointing wage. I had made as much in Gold Basin with a lot less labor.

After ten hours' work my father and I had a mile's walk home. While he milked the cow and fed the chickens, I started the fire and made supper. Then, off to bed for a well-earned sleep. On Saturday we walked the two miles to town for groceries. I roamed the streets while my father had a beer or two, then we had the trek back home. Sundays were reserved for washing clothes and cleaning house. It was a lonely life and a bare existence, with no promise of a better future. Visitors were few and we were too busy or too tired to think of entertainment.

The shingle weavers were making more money than I. If I had to labor to make a living, I wanted to make more money. At the first opportunity I started sawing shingles. With the shingle saw to my left and the clipper saw in front, it was dangerous for anyone. For me, with only one eye, it was doubly so.

Everything went well. I was making almost three times more money than before. I bought a motorcycle and helped my father pay for our home. Everything went well, that is, until the clipper saw cut off my right forefinger. That was all the shingle weaving I wanted to do.

While my hand was healing, I rode the motorcycle a great deal. I became better acquainted with the rest of the state and met many very nice people. My experiences on these trips were very rewarding.

At the mill I had met and liked a young man my own age named Andy Christensen. He was even more alone than I. His only living relative was his father, who roamed the state doing odd jobs. One day Andy asked me if he could go along on my next trip to Everett.

"Sure, Andy, you can ride on the tandem. But what about your job?"

"Oh, I can get a job anytime, or one like it. Let's go."

Andy stayed in Everett while I rode east of the mountains. When I came back several days later, he had found a job he liked better than the one in Granite Falls.

"Why don't you come down here, too," he said. "You're not tied down to any job up there."

"Yes, I know, Andy, but I don't like to leave my father alone."

I rode home with thoughts of going to Everett to live, and wondering how to break the news to my father. I had noticed he had been corresponding with someone in Canada, and I wondered if he was thinking of marriage. Five years had passed since my mother died, so that was a possibility.

One day I asked my father, "I noticed that you have been getting letters from Canada. Are you thinking of getting married?"

"Yes, we are, Elof. Mrs. Anderson and I have been thinking of it for some time, and I have been wondering how I was going to tell you. She is a wonderful person and just as lonesome as I am. She lost her husband and two children some time ago, and I know she would like very much to have a family again."

Things moved rapidly after that. In less than two weeks our place was sold. My father moved to Canada and remarried. I went to Everett and had no problem getting a job I liked in a sawmill there.

I met Andy frequently. He had become acquainted with two sisters, Lottie and Leona Applegate, so we doubledated to dances, shows, and swimming. Andy was the same as I — we were both unsettled and did not want any of these dates to become too serious. Marriage was not in our thoughts yet. I wanted a steady job and a good salary before I took on the responsibility of raising a family.

Epilogue

It was now 1920. Many things had happened in the past years. For myself, those years meant very little in the way of progress. However, they proved one thing: those who have been able to continue their education have reached their goals.

Perhaps, I thought to myself, I have a little less courage, a little less incentive to improve conditions. I could make excuses for my failures. For instance, "If my eyesight had been better . . . or if our mother hadn't died . . ." I could use a number of clichés like, "I've gotten the dirty end of the stick, or a good kick in the teeth, or Fate has handed me a raw deal for being raised on the other side of the tracks." All these were only excuses and solved nothing.

When the war started in 1917, Andy went into the service. I was exempted because of my bad eye. I stayed in Everett, changing from job to job, but not bettering myself. We corresponded occasionally, and when Andy was discharged in 1920 he looked me up.

He was as restless and undecided as I was. He did not want to go to work right away. One Sunday while we were fishing off the dock, he said, "You have talked so much about Monte Cristo. I would like to see it. Let's take a camping trip up there."

I was as eager to go as he seemed to be. Monte Cristo gave me my happiest years and memories. We planned what to take with us. We only had one argument: Andy wanted to take a tent in case of bad weather, and I wanted to take more food. We finally compromised on two oilskin ground sheets. When we had all our things together — the blankets, the cooking utensils, and the food — we had a fifty pound pack apiece.

We took the train only to Granite Falls, since we wanted to walk the rest of the way. Shouldering our packs, we tramped up the tracks out of town. The weather was beautiful. Time was not important. If we saw a nice shady spot or a fishing hole beckoned us, we stopped. Those packs became heavy after a few hours' walking.

We could have ridden on the gas operated rail car, the Galloping Goose I mentioned earlier, but we were on a vacation and wanted to stop whenever we had the notion. The tracks followed the streams so we could fish whenever we saw a good hole. The weather continued good. So far, a tent was not necessary. The ground sheets, however, came in handy — one under us and the other to keep off the early morning dews.

It was a wonderful trip. With every step I felt I was returning to a world I knew and cherished, and leaving problems behind. I kept telling Andy about the various experiences I had had whenever we came to the spots that brought memories to me.

We were camped at the Sunrise mine trail when we had our first threat of rain. The mountain peaks were showing rain clouds. Streaks of lightning flashed from mountain top to mountain top. Luckily, we found some discarded split cedar shakes, and we quickly cut some forked sticks for supports. Leaning the shakes on the supports, we soon had a makeshift shelter. With our ground sheets and our Hudson Bay blankets we would be comfortable.

After supper we crawled into our blankets, and watched the lightning flash across the sky. No rain yet. Just flashes of light and thunder.

Suddenly a tree on the mountain caught fire. It blazed like a huge torch. Then the rains came, but not on us. The peaks were shrouded in mists and rain that put out the fire, and we went to sleep.

During the night I was awakened by something stirring in the bed. While hunting for a match, I woke Andy. He helped me look. "Oh, heck, it's only a toad. Go back to sleep." I didn't want a toad in bed, so I tossed it out in the brush, hoping it wouldn't come back.

The next morning was clear and bright. The smell of coffee awoke Andy. "You got breakfast ready?" he asked. "I'm hungry enough to eat that toad you had in bed last night."

"The bacon is done. The flapjacks will be done by the time you get dressed."

"You know," Andy said. "I'm glad you invited me along on this trip."

We were almost six miles from Monte, or five miles if I could find the short cut through the brush to avoid the railway switchback. I found the short cut. It looked traveled. "Look, Andy. Someone has been traveling here quite often. See, the brush has been cut away. I wonder if someone is living at Monte?"

A half mile further on we saw some buildings. They were strange to me and not in the place where there had been buildings before. I said, "There certainly are some people living here. I wonder what they are doing living here? Maybe they are doing some assessment work on claims."

As we approached the buildings a man came out. It was Jim Kyes!

"Hello," he said. "What are you doing here?"

"I was about to ask you the same thing," I said. "What *are* you doing here?"

"Why, we're mining," Kyes said. "See up there?"

He pointed up the side of Toad Mountain to a tunnel just a couple of hundred feet from where our house used to be. It didn't look like much, but I knew from experience the amount of work and money it took to drill in the hard rock.

"Are you working that ore vein that was under our house?" I asked.

"I am not working that ore vein. I found a very rich mineral deposit on top of old Toad. It is impossible to mine there. I'm drilling now to find it down here close to the tracks."

This was the kind of language I understood. It was something I had heard many times before, not always reporting success. Mentally I wished him good luck, knowing the hopes and expectations he must have.

I said, "Mr. Kyes, you said 'we.' Where are the others?"

"Oh, they're up in the tunnel. They'll come down to lunch soon. They will be glad to meet an old timer who has not forgotten Monte. By the way, how are your folks?" So I told him of my father's marriage in 1915 in Canada, and Ely's marriage in Seattle, and of my own uneventful life so far. Mr. Kyes listened, but made no comment. His greatest thoughts and interest were in his mine, where they had always been.

Before long, three men came out of the tunnel and down to the cabin. We were introduced to the two Andrew brothers and Mr. Ward. They all seemed to have a financial and working interest in the mine. All they could talk about were the prospects and hopes of finding gold. But as I have said, I had heard and seen all that in the earlier days at Monte. The same gleam in the eyes. The same ill-concealed excitement in their voices. To me, it was nothing. Too often I had seen these dreams shattered on the broken ore formations in the mountains of Monte Cristo. Too often I had seen men leave with empty purses and wilted spirits.

Only those who have seen gold glistening in the palm of their hand, free to be picked up off the ground, know the exultation of finding it. This success was not always to be at Monte.

Andy and I stayed several days. We explored the former mines, and took one trip to beautiful Silver Lake. We hunted for some of those sweet, low-growing blueberries among the heather.

I looked with sadness on the smashed homes of the Cooks, the Clevelands, the Hickeys, and the Kimballs. Our home was gone, too. I imagined I could see some of the lumber from our home in the buildings now standing. The old school, the assay office, and Kyes' store were also gone. The Royal Hotel was still standing. Mr. Kyes told us that Mrs. Kyes had been running it for campers and tourists during the summer, but since it now was late September, she had left until next year. It looked very lonely standing among the ruined homes.

The four men toiled in the tunnel and did not have too much time for us. However, I was told that Jim Kyes had started the digging in 1914 with his brother Dan and his nephew Claud Cook. His brother soon pulled out and went into the logging business, and Jim then found his present working partners. With money from relatives in the east, he continued on.

The last evening we were there, we were told news we had not heard before. Dan and Joe Cook, my old schoolmates, were coming up to work for their uncle, Jim Kyes. We were also told of the tragic death of Makinaw Johnson and the Cowden boy, Harry, caught in a snowslide that spring.

Our food was running low, but we did not want to ask Mr. Kyes for any food. They had to get their supplies from Silverton, and we could reach there in four hours ourselves.

When we started out the next morning, the weather was not so good: it was cloudy and promised rain. It was cold, too. The rain began, first mixed with snow, then turning into large flakes, blowing directly into our faces. We could have gone back to Monte, but hated to ask them for any more than the half loaf of bread that Mr. Ward had given us before we started out.

I finally said, "Andy, we had better hurry up fast. There's no telling how bad this storm is going to get." The weather got worse and worse. We could not get lost, or off the track, but we might freeze as we were not dressed for cold weather. As we crossed the bridge over the Sauk River, near Barlow Pass, I suddenly remembered a log cabin that Martin Cummins had built in the woods near this bridge.

"Andy," I said. "There used to be a cabin in the woods near here. I've been there many times. If it is still standing, we can hole up there until the storm is over. I want to look for it." Andy did not want me to go, for fear I might get lost, but I was determined to go. I said, "You stay here and holler once in a while, so I will know where to come back to. If I find the cabin I will holler back and then you come to me. I won't be gone long. If I don't find it in ten minutes or so, I will be back to the tracks." Andy agreed and I left.

The snow was not so blinding in the woods. I found the cabin in less than five minutes. It was as if I had been drawn there by some unknown force. I kept yelling until Andy came.

The rawhide latchstring was still hanging outside the door. As I pulled hard, the crossbar inside lifted and the door opened. I paused to look. It was just as Martin had left it twelve or more years before. His blankets were hung up to the ceiling to keep the mice from building nests in them. The stove was there with wood and kindling nearby, as if waiting for us. We found flour, beans, rice, and oatmeal in tin lard pails. With a couple of lard pails we fixed the partly rusted stovepipe and built a fire.

After cooking some oatmeal mush and later frying flapjacks, we went to bed to save the wood for cooking. It was an eerie feeling to be there with memories of the past. As we lay in the two bunks, I thought of Martin Cummins, that kindly, sometimes drunken Irishman, who had died some years ago. I spoke about the talks we had had in this same cabin many years back. I told Andy of the things old Martin had said to me. Andy listened and wondered, too, about the great urge that made men toil so desperately, seeking that elusive metal called gold. Andy soon slept. I stayed awake longer, thinking about life and what the future had in store for me.

All that night the storm howled, and the snow fell. We were snug and safe, with food and wood to keep us warm. I knew from past experience that storms at this time of year would not last too long, so I did not worry.

In the early morning the weather was much better. A warm rain was falling, and the snow was melting fast. It was noon before we left. We had filled up with food, put out the fire, split wood and kindling, and left everything as we had found it. Once more, Martin's cabin had given food and shelter to wandering travelers. As I closed the door and dropped the latchstring, I had a feeling that he was looking down upon us and wishing us good luck.

With very little snow left, our walk down the track to Silverton was easy. There we caught the Galloping Goose to Hartford, and then the train to Everett. It had been a wonderful trip for us both. For me, Monte would now be a pleasant memory, never quite forgotten, and also a place to visit occasionally.

The next spring, Joe Cook told me of the rock and snow slide that covered the tunnel and wrecked the buildings there. Fortunately, everyone had been at the lower cabin, so no one was hurt.

With funds running low, and with the disastrous slide, the men had to quit. After years of drilling through more than three thousand feet of solid rock and finding no ore, they had given up. That was the end of the Boston American Mine, and an old repeated story of mining at Monte Cristo. Many others had tried with the same results.

Someday tourists and campers will rebuild Monte. With better roads and a new one through Poodle Dog Pass to Garland Hot Springs and Index, people will again have the pleasure of looking at the most beautiful country to be seen anywhere.

Our homes have vanished, crushed by snows.
The tired victims of Nature's blows.
The peaks still stand, so rugged and steep,
Hiding the gold they wish to keep.
    This tale is ended.
    Its errors cannot be mended.
You won't mind any errors you might find.